# Unravelling
# The Spiral

The Life and Work
of Fred Conlon
(1943 – 2005)

Jack Harte

S

Scotus
Press

**For**

*The Conlon family, Kathleen, Orla, Elaine,*
*Niall, Pauric, Finn, Bridie and Nora*

**and**

*for the wide circle of relatives and friends*
*who loved and admired both Fred and his work.*

Published in Ireland by
Scotus Press
PO Box 9498
Dublin 6
Copyright Jack Harte 2010
The moral right of the author has been asserted.

A catalogue record of this book
is available from the British Library.
ISBN 978-0-9560966-1-6

Set in ITC Garamond Book 11pt.


Cover, Design & Layout : Pat Pidgeon
Layout Assistant : Colm McHugh

Photographs
Alan Reevell: 8, 10, 17, 20, 44, 72, 82, 98, 106, 145, 156, 166, 168.
Dept. of Environment, Heritage & Local Government: 14,15.
Jack Harte: 22, 23, 38, 47, 49, 94. Colm McHugh: 33, 69, 111, 131, 148, 152, 157, 163, 167. Joe Haughton: 124. Máire Robinson: 46. Niamh O'Grady: 123. Carrie Conmy: 35. Ronan Conway: 65.
All other phographs from the Conlon Family Archive.

Map: Michael H Phillips:183

# Acknowledgements

I wish to thank many people who helped to make this book a reality. First and foremost, Kathleen, who gave me her time and thoughts and access to all Fred's archives of documents, as well as allowing us to use many of the photographs in the book. Fred's and Kathleen's family, Orla, Elaine, Niall, Pauric, and Finn for their support and interest. Then Fred's two sisters, Bridie and Nora, whose reminiscences brought back our childhood in Killeenduff. Although I eventually decided to write the biography as a personal memoir, I was helped enormously by conversations with many people who were close to Fred as friends, neighbours, colleagues, fellow artists, etc. These conversations helped me to recall incidents more clearly and to ensure that my creative memory was not distorting facts. I include Henry Sharpe, Aidan Hickey, Denis Bannister, John Walsh, Eileen McDonagh, Jackie McKenna, Martha Quinn, Seamus Dunbar, Nuala Maloney, Anita Watts, Eamonn Carney, Willie Lyons, Sean Lavelle and Tommy Lavelle.

Last but by no means least, I want to thank Pat Pidgeon and Colm McHugh of Scotus Press; more than publishers and designers, they have been intimately involved in the evolution of this book as a presentation of Fred's life and work.

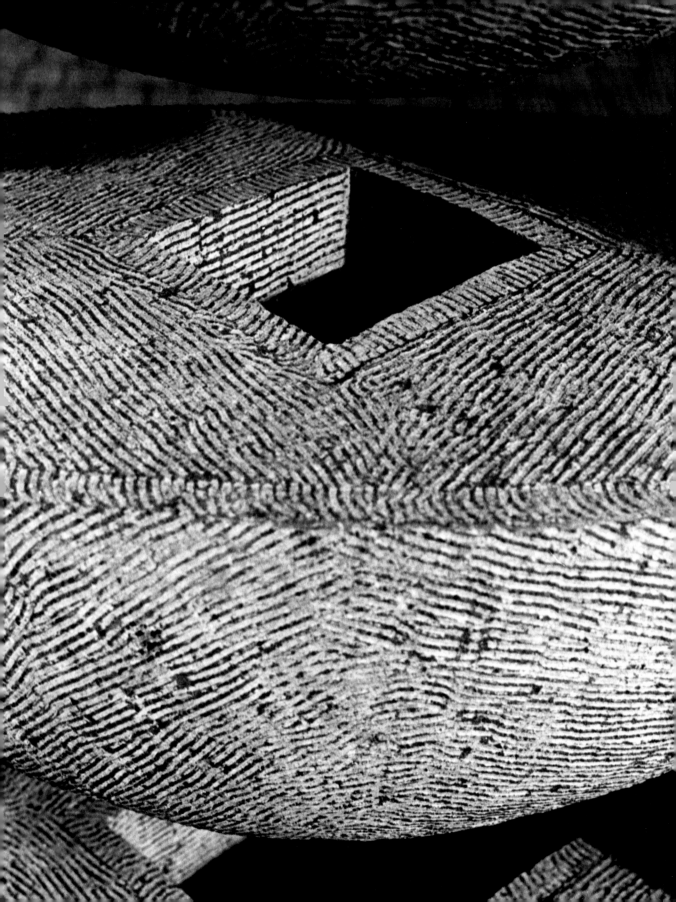

# Contents

*Facing page*:
Detail from
Millennium
Sculpture, Lucan,
Co Dublin

# Chapter 1

# Unravelling the Spiral

On Monday, 17th May, 2004, the sculptor, Fred Conlon, my cousin, next-door-neighbour, life-long friend, took ill; a brain tumour was diagnosed and he was given nine months to live. He died on 24th February, 2005. Despite the diagnosis, despite a family history in which seven of his siblings had died young before him, Fred met the challenge to his life with fierce determination and ferocious optimism. But his physical deterioration was rapid and horrific. A man whose hands had been endowed with all the skill, all the facility, the gods could bestow, struggled to light a cigarette.

I visited him frequently at his home in Tully during his illness and was amazed by his philosophic acceptance of his fate, but also his determination and optimism. He talked about adapting to the new reality: he could no longer carve stone, but he could draw and paint. He could also write, I suggested. And I was not joking: he could express himself extremely well, could even turn a poem, when he put pen to paper. But, as I feared the worst and had an intuition that I would be writing this book one day, I really wanted him to record his views and ideas on art, especially to provide an insight into the creative process behind each of his sculptures. Recognising that he was not able to sustain the act of writing, I gave him a Dictaphone. But he couldn't manipulate the machine. However, Kathleen, his wife, and Orla, his daughter, said they would make a point of recording statements and conversations.

*Facing page*: Detail from Eibhear Alban, Shekina Garden, Co Wicklow

When Kathleen afterwards showed me the diary she had kept over those harrowing months, I found it painful to read. The reflections on art were scant; life and death had taken centre stage. It was an account of day-to-day tribulation, escalating to absolute torture as weeks passed, as his condition worsened, as hope slowly ebbed.

His speculations were more or less what I expected. I knew Fred well enough, after a lifetime of friendship, to be familiar with his thought patterns and his ideas. What I really was expecting now was an indication of his final mindset as he approached death, his final attitude to life and the afterlife. There was one phrase, repeated a few times, which I thought reflected Fred's way of thinking, in a typically symbolic image: 'the second dance of the spiral'. Here are two entries from Kathleen's diary in which he mentions this concept:

5th June … Fred talking …

*I am not necessarily religious. I am a spiritual being, I sense spirituality. I feel lucky to have this sense, I feel the second dance of the spiral brings me into ongoing-ness. This symbol belonged to the ancient Celts, which is meaningful to me now because it brings me into contact with a feeling of flow – the flow of goodness, the greatness of God and the goodness of humanity. Since coming back to Sligo I feel this flow strongly – close family, friends, and strangers. My new learning is wisdom so that I can be gracious. It is all about regeneration, energy flowing back into me and strengthening me. All energy must be put into being positive, no halfway house – the will to survive – the will to get better. Outside of us there is a power greater than all of us. It's pointless asking what went wrong. Even if I knew the answer, it would not make me feel better. If there were burdens, they are yesterday's burdens – All will be well.*

12th June …

*My work has been in conjunction with the spiral. The centre is everything. There is nothing without a point of energy. There is in nature and man a great centre of force. Where this power comes from is the big question. For me, what matters now is to be part of that continuity, the second dance of the spiral. My energies are going into the positive flow. This will give me courage and sustenance. I think of this energy as God. I need to have a power greater than myself.*

At first glance I thought this might be an insight into Fred's vision of the afterlife. But a second glance, at the date, convinced me that, consciously at least, he was still engaging with life itself. He had returned home after his operation and was still determined to get better, still optimistic.

The spiral was one of Fred's favourite motifs. He made explicit and implicit use of it in many of his works. Symbolically, it reflected very well his own approach to spiritual exploration and intellectual investigation, with its dual movement, inwards in eternal introspection, outwards in an openness to others, to humanity, to the world. Alternately, the movement could be seen as down into the local, the personal environment, upwards and outwards towards the universe. Either way, going around the spiral twice appears something of a conundrum.

Fred talks of the spiral as being Celtic, but of course it was carved on to ritual stones long before the Celts, or Celtic culture, arrived in Ireland. It was these sacred stones that haunted his imagination, inspired extraordinary feeling for a material that had gestated in the womb of the earth over millions of years, that had emerged to be shaped and decorated by our ancestors thousands of years ago and by him during his own lifetime.

Fred's use of the spiral was that of the symbolist: the image was symbolic, it represented something more than itself, something deeper, which was not and could not be defined. Yet when the mind meditated on the image it was led on to planes of significance and meaning beyond the grasp of rational thought. And if we follow the path of his exploration, then we will understand a little better the sculptures he based on the spiral, but also gain an insight into the mind and soul of the sculptor. When Fred set down his interpretation of his insight, he related it consciously to God, in the Christian sense, the creative force in the universe, the focal point of his spirituality. But, ironically, if we go further along the path he was following it will bring us back to a pre-Christian concept of God, and to a much better understanding of Fred's subconscious deep spirituality.

So what are these spirals, so popular with our Neolithic ancestors, that inspired so many of Fred's pieces, and that his mind turned to now as he struggled with his fatal illness? And what was he talking about, dancing around the spiral a second time? One conceives of the spiral as a continuous movement, going outwards, or inwards, even in both directions simultaneously – but how does one go around a second time? The first thing we must accept is that, for Fred, the spiral was significant or symbolic, not just a decorative motif. Neither Fred nor the ancients used

motifs solely for decoration. And this motif was prevalent in the artwork of many primitive civilizations.

In order to understand the significance of such a motif to the ancients, it is necessary to shed totally our knowledge of science and the whole databank of information our modern mind has accumulated, using our imagination to project ourselves into the mind of prehistoric man. The ancients looked in awe and reverence at natural phenomena, observed the cycles and processes in nature, and did exactly as we do, tried to make sense of them. Above them their sky was filled with a dazzling array of heavenly bodies that baffled them, but on which they imposed a meaning, an explanation, a concept, so that they could relate to them in a significant way. Of course to them the earth they stood on was the centre of the universe with the heavenly bodies moving around them and their earth in strange irregular but predictable paths.

The most significant of these phenomenal bodies was of course the sun. And our ancient ancestors observed the effect of the sun's heat on the earth and how their very existence depended on it. The sun's rays touching the earth caused growth, enabled life. So they saw the earth as female being fertilized by the rays of the male sun. They studied the annual circuit of the sun and it appeared to them that it followed the path of a

Kerbstone 67 at Newgrange.

spiral (in mathematics a conic helix, because strictly speaking a spiral is two-dimensional, it belongs on a single plane, but we will run with the looser term). To an observer looking south, from the summer solstice to the winter solstice the daily path of the sun, rising and setting, appears to follow that of a spiral moving inwards, from the winter solstice to the summer solstice that of a spiral moving outwards.

When our ancient sculptors put chisel to stone in order to depict this cycle of the sun, they captured it in the spiral image. At first it was a simple single spiral, with loose ends inside and outside, which was of course a depiction of only a half-year's cycle. They also had to address the very different nature of the two half-year cycles. For the first half of the year, the spiral was uncoiling, was creative, giving more and more heat. Then after the summer solstice the cycle was destructive, less and less heat, with growth turning to decay. So they developed a more satisfactory image, a pair of spirals where the moving point starts at the centre of one and maintaining a clockwise movement rotates to the outer ring of that spiral, then swings on to the outer ring of the other and continues in an anti-clockwise direction to the centre of that one (see Kerbstone 67). These counterbalancing positive and negative spirals, with clockwise and anti-clockwise patterns depict the opposition between the Spring/Summer

The entrance stone at Newgrange

creative cycle and the Autumn/Winter destructive cycle. And when the highly sophisticated sculptors who created the entrance stone at Newgrange (see illustration) applied themselves to depicting this annual circuit of the sun, they created a single spiral that moves from a perimeter in towards the centre, converging on a centre point, but then turning around through that centre point and moving outwards again along a parallel path. Again, the movement inwards is anti-clockwise, outwards is clockwise, representing the half year of decay leading to the half year of growth. And if we look at the image as a unit, it is a positive spiral counterbalanced by a negative one, very similar to the yang-yin symbol in Chinese art.

Now, like the sculptors, let us focus on the mystical centre point of this Newgrange spiral (mathematically a Fermat's Spiral). This is the point (which is all the more mysterious and elusive because the movement is continuous) at which the negative changes to positive, anti-clockwise to clockwise. It is the winter solstice. It is the moment when the decay of autumn and winter gives way to the growth of spring and summer.

The Newgrange monument was the basilica of our Neolithic ancestors to this mystical moment in nature. The entrance stone is a sort of marriage stone, festooned with spirals representing the sun superimposed on lozenge shapes, distorted squares, the traditional symbol of earth. At the centre of the monument is a chamber set into a huge mound, and the chamber is accessed through a narrow passage. The chamber is clearly both a tomb and a womb, the tomb of the old negative cycle, the womb of the new positive one. And on the morning of the winter solstice, when the year dies and is reborn, the first shaft of light from the sun makes its way through the passage and fills the inner chamber for seventeen minutes. At its weakest moment the sun penetrates and fertilizes the earth, and the new positive cycle of growth kicks in. This brief intercourse between sun and earth is a mystical moment during which the earth is impregnated, but also during which the sun itself is re-invigorated.

When you appreciate the absolute awe with which our ancestors observed such a natural phenomenon, and the numinous importance they attached to it, you begin to understand the story of St Patrick and the snakes. The abstract mathematical figure of the spiral had zoomorphosed in the imagination of our ancient ancestors into a gigantic snake or serpent or dragon, recoiling and uncoiling in the course of each year, controlling life, benignly bestowing light and heat for half the year, and for the other half

destroying everything it had created. The circular serpent devouring its own tail is a more graphic representation of what the spiral sculptors were representing. But look carefully the next time you see this image, because the serpent is creating itself, emerging from its own mouth, as well as devouring itself.

At face value, Patrick banishing non-existent snakes from Ireland has always appeared a nonsense anecdote, a humorous interlude in the story of the saint's life – and we have always felt a dubious sense of debt to the man for sparing us the nuisance of such vermin that never did make their way to Ireland in the first place. But the snakes that Patrick wrestled with were not real, they were very powerful symbols, they were the spirals that festooned the holy shrines of Pre-Christian Ireland. The great serpent represented the sun, the life force of the universe, the creative ever self-renewing, ever self-destroying power, more or less God. But Patrick's message was that God was personal, not an abstract spiral, not an all-powerful life-bestowing life-devouring serpent. And his snake-banishing feat is echoed in the Christian mythology of most countries, where the founding saint in each case banishes snakes or kills the dragon. Of course Patrick never did succeed in banishing the snakes from Ireland. As they did with everything else, our ancestors retained the old symbols but attached them on to the new Christian message; so the spirals and snakes continued to gyrate even through the decoration on chalices and high-crosses, and we can see them run rampant through that sublime edition of the New Testament, the Book of Kells.

The mystical awe for this moment of renewal in the annual cycle of nature was so deeply and powerfully embedded in the mind and soul of the pagan world that the Christians, instead of trying to quash it, superimposed on it the celebration of the birth of Christ.

As I have said, the spiral was a favourite motif of Fred's. His sense of awe at the mystery of life and at the beauty of nature can best be understood, I think, if we equate it to that which inspired our ancestors to create the Newgrange monument. In his stone sculptures of the spiral, he strives to capture that mystical centre, that turning point where anti-clockwise movement gracefully rotates into a clockwise movement, negative into positive, decay into growth, and as a devout Pagan/Christian he tries to suggest the majestic power of Nature/God manifested in this mystical rotation.

This brings us back to June, 2004. Fred looks at his life, recognizes the signs of physical decline, knows that he still has a huge amount to offer over perhaps another twenty years, and looks with hope and optimism to a mystical turning point in his own life, a force emanating from the centre of the spiral, which will turn decay into growth, negative to positive, and set him on course for the second dance around the spiral.

Wood carving from Fred's College of Art days

# Chapter 2

# Those Early Years

My first encounter with Fred Conlon, that I remember at least, was in a field behind our houses, called Rafter's field. There was a gang of children playing there. I had learned to walk but had never before ventured beyond the confines of my own garden. I remember eyeing the play for a while before making my way into the field to join the fun. I picked out the boy who was closest to me in age, whom I knew to be my cousin, Freddy. (I was called Jackie, and we retained those names in the area until we were grown up.) My experience of approaching Freddy was akin to stepping into the path of a whirlwind. He was all energy and his play dispersed physicality in directionless abandon. I withdrew at some speed. The age difference between, say, 2½ and 3¼, was substantial, but as we grew up the difference dwindled until we were considered, and considered ourselves, the same age!

This was the townland of Killeenduff, near the village of Easkey in Co. Sligo. Fred was born on 14th October, 1943. In the house next door, separated only by a garden wall, I was born ten months later. Yes, we were cousins as well as neighbours, friends as well as cousins. And after the shock of that first encounter had subsided, we grew up together, went to school together, more often than not ate our dinner from the same table.

The two houses had been built by our parents in the thirties on a narrow strip of ground, called the plantation, along the Easkey to Dromore West road. The strip had been woodland before that, left over when the local landlord's estate had been divided, and given in strips to particular tenants as a source of firewood in lieu of a turf-bank. My father's site ran to the corner, the so-called 'Forge Corner', where he set up his own forge

*Facing page*: Detail from 1798 Memorial in Rathdrum, Co Wicklow

The house in
Killeenduff in
which Fred was
born, with my
house next door

to continue the blacksmithing tradition.

Fred's mother, Mary, whose maiden name was Lavelle and was my father's first cousin, had quite an eventful personal history. As a young girl she had moved away from Killeenduff to earn her living as a house servant. One of the places she worked in was Longford House in Beltra, at the Sligo end of Tireragh, famous as the place where Sydney Owenson, Lady Morgan, worked as a governess around 1800, and which inspired her novel 'The Wild Irish Girl' and her collection of essays 'Patriotic Sketches'. The same Cromwellian Settler family, the Croftons, were still in situ, with their aristocratic English titles. Mary Lavelle was not employed as a governess, however, probably in the kitchen or as a chambermaid. She spent time in Dublin too, but I'm not sure when.

She met and married a young man called Francis Wynne. But while she was pregnant with her fourth child, he died of a ruptured appendix. Mary returned to her family in Killeenduff with her children. Her father and brothers built her a small house on the 'plantation' site, the same house in

which Fred was to be born later.

This was in the thirties, when recession was firmly institutionalised, when the Economic War with England was in progress, when poverty was a normal condition for most of the population. Rearing four children on her own at this time was a daunting challenge. But Mary was a determined and very resourceful woman. In her tiny newly-built house she opened a shop to sell items the local community needed such as bread, sugar, sweets, cigarettes. From Dublin she had brought a Singer sewing machine, and offered her services as a dressmaker and seamstress.

She married a second time in 1935, a local man called Pat Conlon. Pat had grown up on his family's farm on the very edge of the sea and still worked on it. But his parents didn't approve of his marrying a widow and the small holding was promptly ear-marked for another brother. So Pat himself had neither land, nor resources, nor a trade of any kind. As a married man with a ready-made family of four children to support, he moved into Mary's house and embarked on the precarious career of the landless

The view from the Forge Corner, the house where I was born in the foreground, Fred's next door

farmer. On Fred's birth certificate he is described as a labourer.

At a time when even a few acres of land provided not only the security of having somewhere to grow your own food crops, but also the essential status of 'owning land', Pat was severely handicapped economically and socially. As a landless farmer he did the exact same work as other farmers, but he had to rent the land he worked. All the holdings were very small, no more than twenty to thirty acres, so the available land was scarce. One year he might have 'conacre', a section of a field, rented from one neighbour, the next year from another. He ploughed, sowed potatoes, oats, barley, turnips, cabbage and other vegetables for household use. And he grew more than he needed for food, in order to have some to sell. He cut turf on the bog and harvested it.

In winter, with other local men, he gathered 'slata mara' or sea rods along the shore, dried them and sold them to a company that extracted

Fred's father and mother, Pat and Mary, outside their house in Killeenduff.

iodine from them. They gathered and sold other seaweeds too, such as car-raigeen and dilisc. And of course winter was the time when storms tossed black wrack up on the shore, which Pat and his neighbours gathered and carted off to fertilise their newly ploughed soil.

It was hard, back-breaking work. Much of it was carried out in isolation or with the involvement of the family. But there was also much swapping of labour – you help me today, I'll help you tomorrow. And of course there were communal efforts, a system called 'the meitheal', where a major undertaking had to be achieved quickly and efficiently. For example, when the threshing machine arrived in the townland it would go from one farm-yard to the next, threshing the cereal crops. It required a team of men, up to perhaps a dozen, to carry out the operation efficiently. So the local men would form a team and move with the thresher from house to house. The effect was that of a carnival, with the activity and excitement, and the

With some of his siblings, left to right, back row Rita, Mary, and Cecil, front Bridie and Fred

spectacle of this great machine gorging on the sheaves of corn, spitting
out the precious grain in a steady dribble. And of course the men had to
be fed in the house where they were working, so the women competed
to outdo each other in generosity. The same happened for hay-making,
bringing home the turf, and other chores that could best be tackled col-
lectively.

Pat Conlon fitted seamlessly into this pattern and system of work,
except that he had the added handicap and indignity of having to rent
land to grow his crops. It was a sore point, and one that festered as time
went by, because when another local estate was being 'striped', divided up
among local farmers, the Land Commission would give Pat not a square

inch on the basis that he did not qualify as a farmer (having no land to start with!).

Back at the house in Killeenduff Pat built stables for a horse and cow. These were grazed on the Cimin, a stretch of commonage along the seashore. The horse was required for the farm-work. The cow provided milk and butter for the family as well as buttermilk for making soda bread. Pat also built a sty for pigs, which he bought as banbhs (piglets) and reared on potatoes, crushed oats, and milk, selling them for slaughter after a few months. At the end of the row of stables was the hen house. Again, the hens were fed on the produce of the land, mostly potatoes and oats, and they provided eggs for the table but also for sale.

But by the time the War broke out, Mary had closed down her little shop. I don't know whether that resulted from the curtailing of supplies through the rationing regime, or whether she no longer had the space in her house. Six more Conlon children were added to the four Wynne boys – a family of twelve in a three-roomed cottage, but that would not have been unusual at the time.

Subsistence living of the type I have described was not exclusive to the Conlon family either. It was the common experience of the vast majority of families. And where some might have the advantage of owning their own twenty acres, the Conlons had the edge in skills, flair, and resource-fulness. I remember the travelling shop coming around the townland, stopping at every house, and Mary would have her surplus eggs, butter, or pots of jam, to barter for whatever groceries she needed. I also remember the Wynne boys being adept at hunting and fishing, so that their staple dinner of bacon and cabbage was frequently replaced by a stewed rabbit or some fried mackerel.

This was the household that Fred was born into. He was the eighth in a family of ten. His four Wynne half-brothers, Patrick, Tommy, Sean, and Francis, were followed by two sisters Mary and Rita, then by a brother, Cecil. After Fred the family was rounded off by his two younger sisters, Bridie and Nora. All of them, except Fred, emigrated, which again was the norm for that generation. Two of them went to the United States, the rest to England. One sister returned later to settle in Northern Ireland, and only in recent years did another sister return to Co. Sligo. By the time Fred was growing up his half-brothers were reaching the going-away age of fifteen or sixteen.

It was a hard-working well-managed family. And like every other boy at the time Fred had to shoulder his share of 'the work', which included the seasonal farming chores, like planting or digging potatoes, weeding drills of turnips, saving hay, harvesting the turf. Coupled with that was the relentless routine of household chores like feeding the pigs and hens, or cleaning out the stables and spreading a bed of fresh straw for the animals.

Next door, I was getting off somewhat lighter. My father, being a black-smith, was not quite so involved in farming. We had no land either and took conacre to grow our own potatoes and vegetables, but just enough for the family. We cut and harvested our own turf, but not the additional cartloads to sell. We kept a cow and hens, and of course I had to take my share of 'the work'. But Fred's burden was always greater, and I would often help him to finish his chores so that we could both get away to hunt rabbits across the fields or explore the rocky seashore.

There were pleasant chores too. Each morning we had to drive our cows down to the Cimin, where they would graze for the day, then collect them in the evening for milking. By dawdling we could avoid a share of heavier chores. In the autumn Fred's mother kept geese, rearing them for the Christmas market. They had to be taken out for a while every day to graze on the 'long acre', the grass along the roadside. On such occasions, the two of us would spend happy hours talking, joking, horse-playing, searching for berries or vetches while we watched the flock of geese nibbling at the way-side grass.

Sunday was the only leisure day, and the only sport available was Gaelic football. Even though I had one of the best football pedigrees in Co. Sligo – my father and my uncle played for the County – I was useless, a great dis-appointment to everyone. But Fred displayed considerable talent, featured on parish teams, and eventually played for Co. Sligo at Minor (Under 18) level. When there was no football we would go fishing, rarely catching any-thing, or hunting rabbits and hares, also rarely catching anything. But we passionately enjoyed exploring the countryside, and knew every field, every ditch, every stone, every clump of furze.

We attended the local National School in Killeenduff, and were in the same class. The teachers were typical of the generation that came of age in the new state: they were fanatically nationalist in everything they did. Even though it was supposed to be an ordinary national school in an English-speaking area, they imposed an Irish-language regime; they con-ducted most classes in Irish, and Irish was imposed as the language of the playground. Their methods of promoting Irish, like their methods of

instruction and discipline, were typical of their time, relying totally on the cane which was administered with unnecessary excess.

Although Fred appeared much tougher, stronger, more resilient than me growing up, he seems to have been affected much more by the random aggression of the classroom. It had little or no effect on me, that I am conscious of, but it seems to have cut deep into Fred's sensibility. One night in a pub in Dublin, when we ourselves had considerable teaching careers behind us, in the course of a chat and a drink, Fred took a sheet of paper out of his pocket.

"I want to read this to you," he said, and proceeded to do so.

It was a long philippic against the instruction methods of the old National schools. Why the need to brutalise children, he asked. Why could the teachers not have empathised with the innocent and impressionable children in front of them, encouraging and nurturing rather than coercing? It was a heartfelt script. And it was evident that the teaching methods in question

Fred considered himself least talented as a colourist, but turned out an occasional landscape. This one shows Ben Bulben, always on our horizon, from his house in Strandhill

had weighed heavily on Fred's mind, that he was unburdening himself by writing this text and reading it to me. I was surprised, having forgotten totally any flaying I had been given. Besides, my experience of two other national schools had made me realise that the teachers in Killeenduff were in no way different from the rest of their generation of teachers. But for Fred, his time at Killeenduff National School represented the greater part of his exposure to formal education. Maybe that was the difference.

So, we can dismiss formal education as an inspiring factor in Fred's formation. More positive was the influence of the community, the way of life, the landscape. The townland of Killeenduff was quite heavily populated at that time. In many of the houses there were large families of an age with ourselves, so we had an abundance of peers to play with, although 'playing' was such a small part of our interaction. In other houses there were unmarried men and women, growing into old age without any children of their own. Yet, in a way, we were their children and they had a role in our lives, like surrogate parents, or benign aunts and uncles. Of course most of them were related to us in some degree anyway.

Many of these were characters, as the word is used colloquially, identified perhaps by a single quality or eccentricity, or even by a single event in their lives. We wandered in and out of their houses as if we were at home. And it was natural to do so – the architectural orientation of the countryside was different then: the road we walked led from house to house and each house opened to the road, unlike nowadays where roads and houses have turned their backs on one another. If the dinner was on the table, and we were hungry, we sat down and shared their food, which was usually no more than a basket of potatoes in the middle of the table. And if we stepped out of line, they reprimanded us.

When Fred was on the last lap of his life, he took nostalgic pleasure in reminiscing about these characters who were our gods when we were growing up in Killeenduff. There were too many to mention separately, but I will give you the example of Daniel's Pat and Daniel's John, two brothers who lived in two houses about a hundred metres apart. Each had his own small farm. Despite being brothers they did not relate to one another at all, passed each other by with a gruff 'hello', that was all.

Pat had gone to America as a young man, but returned to Ireland after being injured in the War, or so we believed. He went around the house and farm with jute potato sacks tied around him, to keep himself warm or clean, or both, but he looked ridiculous. However, when he dressed up on

Sundays, or to go to Ballina on business, he was dapper in the extreme in his spotless suit and black felt hat. We visited him almost every day, probably because he took the time to talk to us, but also because he never failed to have a bar of chocolate for us every time we called. Pat lived in a three-roomed cottage like the rest of us. But the thatched roof on the unused bedroom caved in and Pat withdrew to the two remaining rooms. However, the roof of the kitchen was also thatch, and it too caved in, obviously through lack of maintenance. All Pat did was withdraw to the remaining bedroom with all his furniture. It had a galvanised iron roof and so outlived Pat. It was eerie walking through the part of the house that had no roof because he swept the floor meticulously every day as if he were still living in it, and the bedroom door looked like a bedroom door. Yes, Pat was an eccentric, but to us he was a token of faraway places and distant wars.

His brother, John, looked different and was different, as earthy as the soil he waded through in his turned-down farmer's wellingtons. He kept a bull and had respect and status for providing this service to the townland and beyond. Fred never tired re-telling an experience he had with John. He had visited him on some errand, and John invited him in for a cup of tea. While the kettle was being boiled John put out a cake of bread on the table, explaining that he had baked the cake himself using his own buttermilk. Then he placed a bowl of his own home-made butter on the table. Tea was a great luxury in those years, and so it tasted well despite too much milk and the little globules of congealed cream floating on the surface. They were sitting back enjoying this little feast when a cow came to the front door and peered in. "Ah, that's poor Pruggy now, come to be milked," said John rising from the table. He took up a metal bucket, whereupon the cow ambled right into the kitchen. John drew up a stool, sat in at the udder, and began to milk the cow. When the bucket was about quarter full the cow began spreading her hind legs and arching her back. "Well God blast you anyway," cried John, and with a quick whip he had the bucket in place behind the cow's legs just in time to catch the flow of piss. When he had captured the last dribble, John took the bucket to the open door, dumped out the contents, shook the bucket, returned to his stool, placed the bucket under the cow's udder, and resumed milking. Fred looked at his milky tea with the globules of cream, at the homemade butter, at the bread John made with his own buttermilk, and felt a heave in his stomach. He made a hasty exit and picked a spot to retch. Yes, many times he told that story afterwards. But such were the gods who inhabited our pantheon, who fascinated and moulded us.

Another aspect of the informal education we received from our elders was the transmission of skills. In a society where every man had to do for himself, where no one had the resources to buy services, the skilful one commanded respect and admiration, and had a service to barter. Even if someone was not particularly gifted he had to acquire what were then regarded as necessary life-skills. Older people felt an obligation to transmit skills to children, and children felt obliged to learn them, a process that was ongoing inside and outside the home.

Everyone learned how to mend clothes and mend shoes; the cobbler's last was a fixture in every house. A soldering iron might not be in every house, but could be borrowed if one had a leak in a bucket or basin. Basic building and woodwork skills were traditional, and the services of a qualified carpenter would be engaged only in exceptional circumstances. Butter-making was a routine chore for boys and girls. And so we learned from everyone older than us in the townland. We learned from Mike Maloney across the road how to give a half-decent haircut with his clippers. My father taught us how to pare the hooves of a donkey, and how to hammer home a shoe without nicking the quick. So, if our formal education was an alien experience, our informal education was rich and varied and organic.

The other major influence on both of us was the countryside, the landscape. As children we were free to roam wherever we wished. Whether it was along the rocky coast or through the wooded valley of the Easkey River, the question of danger was never raised as a deterrent. Every natural feature had a proper name which gave it individuality, almost personality. For example, the roads had individual names, the Forge Road, the Wrack Road, the Stirabout Road, the Weasel Road. The fields were pockmarked with mounds and raths, relics of the thousands of years of occupancy by our ancestors, which commanded reverence through the power of folklore and superstition. Thorn bushes and spring wells were similarly imbued with a quasi-religious significance. But the rocks and stones probably had the greatest effect on Fred. There was a dolmen called the Griddle Stone or the Giant's Griddle, indicating its connection to Fionn Mac Cumhaill, very much the hero of local mythology. The countryside was littered with large boulders, erratics deposited by the melting glaciers after the Ice Age, geologists tell us. But such a dry scientific explanation would

not have ignited the imagination of our ancestors, had it been around thousands of years ago. No, it was folklore that explained the existence of these rocks to them, and to us.

For example, in the field right next to our national school stood a huge rock which was cleft down the middle. The Split Rock was a landmark in every sense. Houses and boundaries and roads could change, but the Split Rock stayed the same. People gave directions by it – our houses were a couple of hundred yards beyond the Split Rock. As children we looked at it in awe. It was said that if you attempted to go through the cleft three times it would close in and squash you like a bug. That made it more alluring, and we could scarcely pass by without feeling the pull of its ominous invitation. Its origins were explained thus. Fionn Mac Cumhaill and another giant warrior were standing on top of the Ox Mountains. They challenged one another to a stone-throwing contest. Fionn's rival took up a boulder and

The Split Rock in Killeenduff, Co. Sligo. The national school we attended was just behind the trees

33

hurled it towards the sea. It landed right on the foreshore. Fionn took up a similar sized rock and hurled it with all his might, expecting to see it drop into the ocean. But it fell about a mile short. Fionn rushed down in fury and when he reached the boulder he struck it with his sword, slicing it cleanly down the middle. (In some versions he hit it with his little finger – Ireland's first karate chop!) In later years when I heard Fred talk of the mystery and magic and allure of a piece of sculpture, I fancied he could have been talking about the Split Rock.

In March 1953, when I was eight years old, my family left Killeenduff, and moved to Lanesboro in Co. Longford. My father's trade was in decline because horses were being replaced by tractors on Irish farms. The farm implements he had fashioned were being cast aside, and mass production was making available at a lower cost many of the items the smith had heretofore provided. So he closed the forge and got a job with Bord na Mona, a company set up by the government to exploit the bogs for the commercial production of peat fuel.

Our move to the Midlands meant that my path and Fred's diverged for the first time. However, each summer without fail I returned to Sligo, sometimes by myself, sometimes with my whole family, sometimes staying with other relatives, sometimes in Fred's house, sometimes staying with the rest of my family in our own cottage next door to Fred. But, wherever I was lodging, I spent the endless daylight hours as before, loitering about his house or helping him with his chores in order to buy the freedom to wander the countryside from the mountains to the sea.

It was during one of those summer holidays that the two of us went into the village of Easkey. We were around twelve or thirteen years old. I was looking for picture postcards of Sligo to bring back with me. Eileen Mary Harte, no relation, had a souvenir and craft shop in the village, and while I was going through her postcards, Fred took up one of her 'souvenirs', a little thatched cottage, and examined it.

"You know, that's not very good," he said to Eileen Mary. "I could do better than that myself."

"Are you serious?" said she. "Well, do you want to try?"

Fred was as surprised by her response as she must have been by his brash claim. But she went into a back room, and re-emerged with a packet of plasticene.

"Now," she said. "Take this home and see if you can make me a better cottage."

It was an exciting challenge, and we headed straight home to Killeenduff. Across the road from our two houses was a perfect example, a thatched cottage, a house we loved, one of our rambling houses. Fred started working the plasticene, modelling Maloney's house. A gate opened from the roadside into a small garden and a short path led up to the front door. All of this Fred incorporated into his model, then had the bright idea to turn the whole thing into an ashtray, using the garden as the tray and the gate as the cigarette holder. The result was an authentic reproduction despite the change of function.

The very next day we were back with Eileen Mary, and she looked impressed, absolutely clucking with compliments.

"Come back to me in a couple of days and I'll have something to show you," she said, without elaborating.

We were intrigued as to what she intended and duly returned a couple of days later. When she saw us enter the shop she went into the back room and returned holding a tray on which were arranged about a dozen copies

This old damaged photo was taken on one of my family holidays back to Killeenduff. Myself and Fred are on the extreme right, his mother and two sisters, Bridie and Nora, are on the extreme left, and my father in the centre, on whom Fred modelled the Blacksmith (Draíocht an Ghabha)

of Fred's cottage, his ashtray, in gleaming white plaster.

We marvelled. She preened in delight at our amazement.

"Are you as good at painting as you are at modelling?" she asked Fred.

"I don't know. Why?"

"Well, if you take these away and paint them, I'll put them on sale and we'll divide the takings between us."

Fred's face was lit up, even through the mist of bewilderment. This was no longer child's play. This was serious business. Doing something for which you were paid, in cash, was rare, even among the adults in our community.

We made our way back to Killeenduff, Fred carrying the box of neatly packed plaster reproductions, I carrying the bag of paints and brushes Eileen Mary had given him.

"How did you know you could make the cottage?" I asked him.

"I don't know why, but I just knew. It was a sort of feeling," he said. "Did you ever have that sort of feeling?"

I laughed. "Yeah, I have the feeling that I couldn't do the simplest thing with my hands, even if I was at it for a hundred years. I have two left hands. But I always have the feeling that I could write a poem."

"Did you ever try?"

"No, never. That's the funny thing."

"Maybe now is the time to have a go."

"Yeah, maybe it is."

And so began what I have often, jokingly, referred to as the 'cottage industry', Eileen Mary reproducing the model in plaster, Fred painting each one by hand. And they were selling. It was a commercial success, and Fred was earning money for the first time in his life. When they had exhausted the market for thatched cottage ashtrays, they moved on to Blarney Castles, and Celtic Crosses. To facilitate him, his mother gave him an old dresser for his array of paints and materials, and a corner of the kitchen to work in.

There was no limit to this spontaneous eruption of his artistic exuberance. In his kitchen there was a cupboard with two large doors. On one of these he painted a picture of the Blessed Virgin, on the other a picture of Jesus as the Good Shepherd. These pictures were the wonder of the townland and people called in regularly to see and admire them. They declared that they were better pictures than any you could buy even in a shop in Knock. My aunt, who was a religious devotee, commissioned him

to do a drawing of the Pope, John 23rd, and it hung on her wall for the rest of her life.

Every summer there were Agricultural Shows throughout the County. Generally the interest was in the competitions for livestock and farm produce, but they also had a section for crafts. Fred entered paintings, mainly landscapes, in these shows, and we travelled to each location on our bicycles with competititve zeal. Occasionally they would have competitions for poems or photographs, and I would have something to enter. As far as I remember, the prize for each competition was a rosette. I never won a rosette, but Fred had enough to paper his walls.

One day we were at Sligo Agricultural Show, admiring a painting by a rival competitor. When a young man beside us overheard the complimentary remarks, he indicated proudly that the painting was his. He was a few

The thatched cottage ashtray. This copy belongs to Anne Taylor, Ballina, who received it as a present all those years ago

Fred left, and myself, aged 15 or 16, pretending to be drunk! Note the cupboard doors on which he had painted Jesus and Mary

years older than us, but Fred and he launched into an animated conversation, complimenting each other on their works, analysing them, comparing their artistic experiences. When the young man mentioned that he had been to Dublin and visited the galleries there, Fred was wide-eyed with admiration. "And did you see any paintings by Yeats?" he asked. "I did, and I wouldn't give tuppence for the lot of them. Every one I saw was a slobbering mess. I couldn't make head nor tail of what he was trying to paint."

Then the two of them fell silent, as it were, basking in the satisfaction that they could fashion a recognisable picture, unlike poor Yeats who did his best but didn't quite manage it.

There is no explanation of Fred's sudden interest in, indeed obsession with, art in terms of external influence of any kind. There was not an iota of art on the curriculum of the National School. Until the encounter with Eileen Mary there was no art-related activity in the locality that might have sparked his interest. There was certainly no art, nor artists, nor artistic awareness, in any of our families. Life in Killeenduff was, as I have portrayed, a continual struggle for survival by grinding through the chores daily, weekly, seasonally. And even though Fred's talent was encouraged and assisted at home, he was not given an exemption from the mundane graft.

By the time he was leaving the National School, many of his older brothers and sisters had emigrated. His father and mother were taking a quiet pride in his achievements and his talent, which surprised and perplexed them too, but which marked him out in the community as someone special. With the greater part of their family reared, they were becoming more relaxed also. At least that was my impression, but then they were also getting older, slowing down, and partial to those long easy conversations around the range in the kitchen, conversations I enjoyed enormously. In this atmosphere exuding new-found contentment, it was possible to reflect on the good times and the bad times with equanimity.

Mary was an extremely able woman, but I am certain that never for a moment did she think so of herself. Fred thought she had a deep sense of self and self-worth which gave her that confidence to tackle any task and succeed, but without swagger, without betraying whether she even reflected on her achievement. She was certainly a perfectionist constantly preaching, "If you are going to do something, do it well, or else don't bother doing it at all." She also had what we would now call 'taste'. She never discarded anything she valued, always recycling or finding a new use for old things. Her skilfulness and imaginative using of materials are the only, albeit slight, external source of Fred's early inclination towards the visual arts.

Like many women, and men too, of her generation she was deeply and intensely spiritual with an unquestioning devotion to Catholicism. Yet never for a moment did she appear 'pious'. On the contrary, she had an earthy sense of life, and a wicked sense of humour. And she could laugh at herself too. For example, many times the story of Fred's 'birthday present' was retold around the range, and she would laugh at it as heartily as everyone else.

It went like this. One evening, Fred went to collect the cow from the Cimin for milking. For whatever reason, he dawdled. He may have encountered some playmates, or gone exploring the seashore, or brought a notebook with him to sketch the outline of the Castle. Mary was waiting impatiently for the cow so that she could do the milking quickly, because she had to go to the village afterwards. Fred was particularly tardy that evening, and when he arrived through the gate driving the cow in front of him, her frustration got the better of her. Out she went, and with a perfectly aimed kick she connected with his backside. A few days later, a neighbour of ours, a couple of years older than us, Martin Connolly, called in to Conlons. He had a pair of shining new shoes on. "Did you get new shoes, Martin?" asked Mary. "I got them for my birthday," said Martin. "Today is my birthday and Aunt Belinda in America sent the money home for them." "They're very nice," said Mary. "Well wear." Then Martin realised that Fred's birthday had been a few days earlier. He turned to Fred. "What did you get for your birthday, Fred?" Fred exploded. It was as if he were waiting for this opportunity. "The only shoe I got for my birthday, Martin, was a shoe in the arse." And Mary was mortified, realising that the incident of the cow had happened on his birthday. But in those days there was little sentimentality about birthdays, and many in Mary's generation had no idea on what day of the year they were born.

But behind Mary's tough exterior, behind the shield of hardness she thrust in front of her to take the bullets of the world, there was an enormous core of warmth and gentleness and generosity. In her business dealings with other people she was imbued with the value of decency, a value that underpinned rural culture of the time – if she couldn't do you a good turn, she certainly wouldn't do you a bad one. To her close friends she was the very embodiment of generosity. I remember being overwhelmed one summer when I had been staying in her house, or at least, as usual, having my meals there. The day I was leaving to go back to the Midlands, she called me aside and slipped a ten-shilling note into my hand. I was stunned. It was a huge amount of money then, relative to what people had. It would be at least equivalent to someone tipping a kid fifty euro today.

Mary's health was never robust, and almost every year she was wracked by a bout of illness, usually described as pleurisy, which kept her confined to bed for weeks on end. One of my chief concerns, reaching Killeenduff each summer, was for Mary's health. Life was considerably duller when she was reduced to a coughing presence in the upper room.

Fred's father Pat was a perfect foil to Mary. Despite the rigours of his life as a landless farmer, he had the reputation for being 'easy-going', no doubt because of his relaxed manner and his out-going sociable personality. He was tall, with a well-honed physique, but his open face and jovial eyes always invited conversation. And how he loved conversation. No matter how intense were the demands on his time, he would pause to talk. Of course winter was the best time to catch him, when time was a plentiful commodity.

He would sit back then by the fire and reflect on life, for hours on end, always emphasising each declaration with his own personal oath, "as sure as you're a foot high". He was an extremely warm-hearted man who took great pride in his family, and in Fred's achievements, but of course would never say that in so many words. He and Mary were well matched, comfortable in the traditional roles, where the husband looked after the farmwork, and the woman was the home-maker, the family accountant, the manager of the children.

When he left the national school in 1957, Fred proceeded to Easkey Vocational School, or the 'tech' as it was affectionately called. In those days many children ended their formal education on leaving the national school.

The Vocational Schools, administered directly by the state, were limited to a brief of preparing boys and girls for work, particularly for apprenticeships. They were not allowed to provide courses for the Intermediate and Leaving Certificates in competition with religious-run secondary schools. Instead, they provided a two-year course for the Group Certificate, and had the option of preparing students for additional work-oriented examinations. Fred did the Group Certificate after the normal two years and then stayed on for an optional third year.

There was no art on the programme at Easkey Vocational School, which consisted of Irish, English, Mathematics, Woodwork, Mechanical Drawing and Rural Science. Nevertheless, he enjoyed the 'tech', and responded to the humane attitude of the teachers. He would often sing their praises to me, recounting whole lessons in Woodwork with Joe McHugh, the Principal, or in Rural Science with Gerry Danaher. The practical orientation of the subjects suited him too and boosted his confidence in his own ability.

The regime in the Vocational School was flexible and tolerant, recognising that boys of that age were going to be kept at home for the major seasonal jobs, appreciating that families were making sacrifices to keep them in school beyond the age of compulsory attendance, fourteen. On the other hand, the students were not attending in order to acquire a liberal education, but to acquire whatever qualifications were needed for an apprenticeship or a similarly better grade of employment.

Within this framework Fred spent three happy years. He did not flaunt his talent, nor his passion for art. But he was not averse to displaying his skill occasionally and one day astounded his classmates and teacher by drawing a picture of the Blessed Virgin. This was much admired and much talked about, and yet Fred was not regarded as a freak: after all, he was one of the best players on the Gaelic Football team, was capable of enjoying horseplay like everybody else, teased and courted the girls who, although attending the same school, were kept in modest isolation from the boys.

Fred's 'cottage' project was seen by the family as such, as a little side-line which brought some cash into the home and kept Fred in pocket-money for the three years he spent in the Vocational School. By the time he finished in 1960, there seemed little prospect of his project leading anywhere. However, Fred was becoming more and more dedicated to art. He resisted the pressure and the temptation to take the boat to England like everyone else. And Eileen Mary Harte had a zealot's belief in his exceptional talent. So, while Fred punched in another year producing plaster souvenirs, she embarked on a campaign.

First, she went to Joe McHugh, the Principal of the Vocational School, and declared that Fred's talent was such that it would be irresponsible to stand idly by and see it neglected, that mountains should be moved, if necessary, to have it developed properly. Joe was in total agreement and enthusiastically pledged his support.

Eileen Mary's aim was to have Fred study in the National College of Art in Dublin. Even the recitation of the name of such a remote and august institution filled us with awe and terror. Not only did it seem unattainable, it was even beyond the sphere of our comprehension. But she was a formidable lady. Mountains had to be moved, and she was going to bulldoze them.

She and Joe paid a visit to the CEO of Co Sligo Vocational Educational

Committee, Tom Mac Evilly, and showed him some samples of Fred's work. He was a sophisticated and enlightened educationalist, and he was impressed. What they wanted was a scholarship for Fred to enable him to study at the National College of Art for the full period of five years. The problem was that there was no such scholarship in Co Sligo. There was no such scholarship in any other county either as far as Tom Mac Evilly was aware. The only scholarships for Third Level education at the time were the much prized County Council University Scholarships awarded on the results of the Leaving Certificate Examination, at the rate of three per county, or so.

However Tom Mac Evilly became totally converted and committed to the cause. He examined the rules and the regulations, the laws and the bye-laws governing the Vocational Educational Committee and discovered some rule which would allow the Committee to create such a scholarship in exceptional circumstances.

So a meeting was arranged at which the Committee would interview Fred. They gathered up all the samples of his work, the plaster souvenirs, the drawings, the paintings – they even took the doors off the cupboard on which he had painted Mary and Jesus – and brought them all to the interview.

And yet it was all unreal. Dublin was another world. The National College of Art was daunting, even in its title. The prospect of a young fellow from Killeenduff, son of a landless farmer, with no education beyond the Group Certificate, whose life experience had been limited to endless farm work, going to the National College of Art was unthinkable, unimaginable.

And yet it happened. The Committee interviewed Fred, looked at his work, and agreed that he was exceptional. So they instituted a scholarship specially for him, exactly on par with the University Scholarships, and Fred was off to the National College of Art in Dublin in the autumn of 1961.

# Chapter 3

# The Dublin Years

I arrived in Dublin during the summer of 1963 to work down on the docks where the ships came in with grain. I had done the Leaving Certificate and was hoping to have won a University Scholarship. Country people coming to Dublin in those days relied on the family network for support, so I was staying with my Uncle, Tony Foley, out in Walkinstown.

Of course I linked up with Fred immediately. He had spent the two years since he came to Dublin with another uncle of mine, Henry Foley, who lived with his family down in Sheriff Street. But for the summer Fred was staying in a garret overlooking the canal. He was minding it for a friend and fellow student who had gone off to work in England for the summer. The sight of Fred in this light-filled attic, with guitars and books strewn around, instantaneously impressed on me that he had moved into a new phase. And so had I.

He made mugs of coffee for me and talked non-stop about Dublin, and art, his new life, and art, his friends, and art. After the Preliminary first two years in the College, Fred had opted to specialize in sculpture. He had gradually discovered his real artistic talent and had gravitated toward that department, working under Domhnall Ó Murchadha, the Assistant Professor of Sculpture, whom Fred and everyone else called Murphy. The Professor was a German sculptor named Herkner, but Fred dismissed him with a shrug of the shoulders. Murphy was the presiding spirit in the school of Sculpture. Fred was wildly enthusiastic about Murphy in whom he discovered a perfect mentor, a kindred spirit, a surrogate father.

Murphy had a private studio down in Percy Place, just off the Grand Canal, a short walk from the bohemian garret Fred was living in. He had a

*Facing page:*
Detail from Cois
Cuan, Boyle,
Co Roscommon

The right-hand panel over the entrance to Galway Cathedral, sculpted by Domhnall Ó Murchadha. The figure holding the book was modelled on Fred, who assisted Domhnall on this commission

few large commissions on hand and had employed Fred for the summer holidays to work on these projects. It was on a Sunday that I had called in, so after the numerous cups of coffee, a beverage we were totally unfamiliar with in the country, we set out for the studio. It was closed for the day, of course, but Fred had the key.

So this was what a studio looked like. It was no corner of heaven, no epitome of romance. It was a large shed, cluttered with artefacts, benches, and tools, all heavily powdered with grey dust. The atmosphere was of a work-place, like a mechanic's garage, like my father's forge. Then Fred began to point out things to me. First there was the large relief panel they were working on, one of a series commissioned for the new cathedral in Galway. It looked formidable. Murphy had given Fred specific tasks to work on. It sounded like the relationship of master and apprentice in the studios of the Renaissance artists. And Murphy had modelled one of the disciples in this relief on Fred.

Then he showed me some crumbling plaster figures put aside in the corner of the studio. Fred was practically holding his breath, and his voice quavered as he spoke about these crumbling derelicts. These, he said, had been modelled by Jerome Connor, and I sensed by the reverence in his tone that Jerome Connor, although unknown to me, was a name to be revered. One figure was an angel, standing on a plinth, her foot emphatically stamping on a sword, and underneath was an inscription, 'Siothcáin i n-ainm Dé'. This figure was for a memorial to the people who drowned on the Lusitania when it was torpedoed off the Cork Coast during the First World War, Fred explained. Connor was commissioned to do the memorial for Cobh by American donors, but before he could complete it, the money dried up, probably as a result of the Great Depression in the United States.

"Look at that figure", he said. I looked. It was a very beautiful young woman dressed in an old-fashioned gown. "Can't you see every inch of her body, every muscle and sinew underneath the drapery? It's as if he started with the nude figure and covered it afterwards." I could see what he meant. The drapery was not hugging her figure, but the figure glowed under the folds of cloth. "Look at the bodice," he said. "Can't you almost feel the tautness in the thong that laces the two sides together?" Fred was almost breathless with excitement. "And look at the wings." He ran his fingers over the undulations of the feathers in the two wings that circled her body, not quite spread but not wholly at rest either. "Beautiful". And when he raised his fingers I could see they were covered in powder and flake. "That's what I'm working on when I'm not helping Murphy. Restoring the plaster." I looked closely and saw how the holes in the flaking crumbling plaster were being filled in with fresh solid plaster. I stood back to admire. The angel had two outstretched hands curling upwards as if imploring peace. It was magnificent.

Fred then drew my attention to another one. "We call it Mother Ireland, but it's supposed to be a memorial to the Kerry Poets." It was again a beautiful figure of a woman seated, one elbow resting on her knee with the hand supporting her chin, the other arm stretched over a harp the strings of which were sundered. "When we are finished the angel we will be starting on this."

"Who is Jerome Connor?" I asked. That was cue enough for Fred to launch into an impassioned account of the life and work of an artist who was clearly firing him with enthusiastic inspiration. Although born and reared in Anascaul, Co. Kerry, Connor had emigrated to the United States as a young man and had become a leading sculptor of public monuments over there. After the Irish Free State was set up in 1922, Connor returned to Ireland hoping to celebrate the emergence of the independent nation in bronze monuments. At first the commissions did come, but after the collapse of the American economy in 1929, the money dried up. The commissions did not get the support he was expecting in Ireland either, and stalled. Eventually he went bankrupt. The plaster figures that were ready to be cast in bronze lay mouldering in his studio after his death in 1943, until Murphy rescued them. They were now going to restore them and ensure they were cast and put in place.

"Fair dues to Murphy," I said. "He must be some man."

"He is," agreed Fred. "You'll like him too. He's full of stories and steeped in Irish culture. He's someone you could listen to all day. We might catch him later in the Gallery. His wife is Máirín Allen and she's an art historian. She gives a lecture in the National Gallery every second Sunday, and I know she's on today."

He closed the studio and we walked across the delightful bridge over the canal at Upper Mount Street, past the quaint Peppercannister Church, down streets of Georgian facades, to Merrion Square. We strode with the buoyancy of youth and hope and ambition, with a sense of work to be done, goals to be achieved, and a universe of knowledge to be explored. It was good to be in Dublin.

Inside the Gallery Fred lowered his voice, as if we had entered a church, but continued talking. "This is all rubbish," he nodded his head at a long room, packed with paintings. "The English can't paint. Blake was the only painter they had." He quite took the breath from me with that sweeping dismissal of a sizable display in the National Gallery, and I wondered whether he had been told that by Murphy, or whether he had worked it out for himself. "The Irish are no better," he added, perhaps to show that his judgement was not on chauvinist grounds. "What about Yeats?" I asked, anxious to find out if his work was a 'slobbering mess'. "I'll say this much for Yeats," he replied, still whispering, "he could draw. His early work is not bad."

We came to a room where the lecture was in progress. We slunk in to sit on two chairs at the back, but Máirín Allen paused for a second and smiled as she caught sight of Fred. "This is the French Room," he whispered. "This

48

is where the real paintings are." She was standing in front of Poussin's 'Entombment of Christ', her finger waving about, pointing out the extraordinary realism of the corpse, the geometric pattern of the design, the heroic quality of the figures, the balances in shapes and colours. When she finished, her audience began to shuffle off, but we waited and then went up to talk to her.

She struck me as a warm bright woman, what we would have called in Sligo, 'homely', and she clearly liked Fred. Presently Murphy arrived to collect her. He was tall and dark-featured, soft spoken, and, for a man to whom one could listen all day, he didn't say much. We took our leave.

Going down the wide marble staircase, Fred greeted a fellow student who had a sketching pad and a pencil. He was studying painting in the College. After a few bantering exchanges, he suggested we go to the Coffee Inn. There we eked out coffees to accommodate conversation until we started to attract disgruntled glances from the portly flabby-faced owner. We left the Coffee Inn and took the short walk to Grafton Street. On Fred's insistence we entered the Grafton Cinema, paid a shilling each, and watched non-stop cartoons for the rest of the evening. With Fred and his friend roaring with laughter at the antics of the Roadrunner and Donald Duck, I relaxed into the cushioned seat, reflecting that I was now in Dublin, inducted into the world of art students.

* * * * *

Fred settled into the Sculpture specialization that autumn with great enthusiasm and satisfaction. Having had a taste of the independence of the attic room during the summer, he had joined with a fellow student in the Sculpture Department, John Walsh, to rent a double bedsitter. Accommodation was in great demand in Dublin, because of the influx of young people from the country, as students or as workers, and consisted of digs, single bedsitters, or double bedsitters. Almost all options were dreadful by today's standards and were relatively expensive. John Walsh had spent the previous year in a tent up in the Dublin mountains.

I had won my County Council Scholarship to the University, but my university education lasted only six weeks. By then I had done the arithmetic and realized I would survive only until Christmas, even with the indulgence of my uncle and his family. So I looked for a job and got one in the Civil Service, which was going through a phase of taking all comers. And

I marvelled at how Fred was managing to survive on his scholarship money.

I was now installed in a bedsitter in Harcourt Street, which was also an attic room, but small low and narrow, resembling a coffin with one window in the narrow end wall.

The one Fred and John had was a bit more spacious, a large room with two single beds, a cooker and a sink. It was in Wellington Road in Ballsbridge, not far away.

I visited one Saturday afternoon, carrying my packet of chocolate gold-grain biscuits which had become de rigueur for having with the coffee. Although Fred was expecting me, there was no response to the doorbell. Another tenant was coming out, so I slipped inside and knocked on the door of the room. There was a shuffling inside and a delay before John's voice came softly through the door, "Yes?"

"Jack here. I'm calling for Fred."

"Oh!"

There was some more shuffling, before the door was finally opened.

Inside were three others besides Fred and John, and there was a strange atmosphere of tense amusement. Amid giggles and efforts to keep straight faces, I was introduced to the three I hadn't met before, Henry Sharpe, Aidan Hickey, and Donal Byrne. I was mystified as to what was going on until Henry Sharpe eventually spoke up in his forthright way.

"I'm sure you're wondering what the hell is going on, and what the five of us are doing lurking in the room. We were having a life-drawing session, and the landlord has been prowling about since he saw us arriving. He probably thinks we're having an orgy. When you rang the bell John was sure it was he, and was trying to shush us up."

They all burst into laughter again, all except John, who looked uncomfortable. He was obviously afraid of having to go back to the tent in the mountain.

"Life-drawing?" I asked, trying to appear casual.

And while Fred filled the kettle and put it to boil on the black gas cooker they all started talking in intensely animated tones. The life-drawing class in the College was a fiasco, totally inadequate. It was as if the College were apologetic for having to put it on at all. As for the models, they had the attitude that they were doing an enormous favour by taking off their clobber at all, and sulked, and refused to pose as requested. Donal mimicked the female model and they all laughed in merry recognition. So they had got together and decided to have their own sessions, one person in turn acting as model each time. I looked around at them quite dumbfounded. Sitting looking at a nude model in the College of Art was something that outsiders joked about, hardly believing that art students could be so lucky. Dismissing it, as they did, astonished me. Having to draw male models, however, appeared distasteful. But to model, nude, for all your friends, taxed the sense of utter inhibition I still carried from my rural childhood. Listening to their determination to overcome whatever barriers needed to be overcome in order to develop their skills detonated a charge deep in my mind: these people were out of the ordinary, these people were inspirational.

While we sat around on the beds or squatted on the floor drinking coffee and eating chocolate biscuits, I focused on formulating an impression of the three new people I had just met. Henry Sharpe had a full black beard and a gravelly voice but articulated his words with precision as if even the most trivial remark was carefully thought out. They joked about his being an atheist, but a Protestant atheist, as opposed to the rest that were common or garden Catholic atheists. All except Fred. Fred was still a regular church-goer and went quiet when Catholicism was being lambasted. Henry was also singled out by his enthusiastic commitment to abstract painting.

Aidan Hickey was the left-winger of the group, also bearded. He was quiet spoken but none the less confident in his opinions. When he heard I had moved into a bedsitter in Harcourt Street, he asked me if there were any more vacant. He was from Malahide and still lived at home, but wanted a place in town as he now had a few hours teaching out in Tallaght which was on the opposite side of the city from Malahide. I told him there probably was as the house was huge and divided into so many small bedsitters it looked like a warren. "I don't mind small as long as it's also cheap", he replied. I invited him to come back with me and check with the landlord.

Donal Byrne was clean shaven, dapper, clever with repartee, and appeared to be extremely well read and well versed, my idea of what an intellectual must be. When Fred mentioned, much to my consternation, that I wrote poetry, Donal asked my opinion on particular poets. Not only had I not read them, I had never heard of them.

I was quite overwhelmed by the lively verbal fencing of these people, the evidence of erudition in their well articulated arguments, and the serious

Head of a girl
that Fred
modelled in the
College of Art,
displayed in the
College yard

Another example
of his clay
modelling in the
College of Art

commitment to art that galvanized their conversation. I felt the weight of my own inadequacy. I was outside the dynamic of this animated brotherhood, but Fred was very much central to it. It was evident that he was deeply respected, and when he expressed an opinion it was weighed up with total seriousness.

Yes, I felt like an outsider, but they didn't seem to regard me as such. They had organised a seminar on Art and Philosophy and invited me to come along. The philosophy side was being provided by a priest acquaintance of Donal's and he would probably be supported by some philosophy students from Opus Dei. The venue would be the Opus Dei house in Ely Place.

"Opus Dei?" I asked. "That's an unlikely venue for a meeting of atheists."

"I'm sure they are hoping to save our souls", said Donal. "But there's a danger we might drag them into damnation."

On the way back to Harcourt Street with Aidan, I asked him about Fred, an exploratory question to divine how he stood in the estimation of his peers. Fred was quite extraordinary, according to Aidan. He had an amazing visual sense. If someone had a problem with say a painting or a drawing and couldn't determine what was wrong he would ask Fred to have a look at it. With a glance Fred would be able to identify the problem and suggest solutions. Yes, my cousin was highly regarded by his peers.

The more I got to know them, the more I realised how much Fred had in common with this circle of friends. They were all from working class backgrounds and in those days art was not the preserve of the underprivileged. Parental pressure at that time was very much towards attaining secure employment, and art was not identified as secure employment. Each of them came to art out of a passion they discovered within themselves and even though this would have perplexed or even alarmed their families, there was clearly moral support for what they were doing. They were all surviving at the subsistence end of the economic spectrum, so there was no money for drink or luxuries of any kind. When they went in to the College every morning they had to be sure of having the few pennies required to buy paper for the day's drawing or painting exercises. Their only concession to security aspirations was their general intention to gain the qualifications for teaching.

Unlike Fred and John, who were very happy with the sculpture department and with Murphy's mentoring, the others were generally unhappy with the painting department. Donal had been thrown out of the painting classes after an argument with the lecturer, and Aidan and Henry had left the department, but there was this strange dispensation whereby a registered student could go in every day and use the facilities and attend whatever classes they wished. And they did just that.

Much of their art education came from books and magazines; through these they educated themselves and gained familiarity with past masters and contemporary developments. So, after hours of reading in the National Library they would repair to the Coffee Inn to dissect the theories of Ruskin, or Herbert Read, or Bernard Berenson.

* * * * *

The bedsitter life did not suit Fred, whatever about John. They did not eat well or regularly and dissipated their money on ephemera, so that they were constantly broke when they needed to pay for food or electricity. Fred consulted my Aunt Kathleen, wife of Henry Foley, with whom he had stayed for two years, and she found him digs with an old lady called Mrs McGinn. It was a match made in heaven, as they say. Mrs McGinn had a little artisan's cottage in a terraced cul-de-sac off Seville Place. She was elderly, but lively, jolly, earthy, a typical Dublin woman, as Fred declared. She was a widow and had no children of her own but she was the quintessential motherly type. And how she took to Fred and how she mothered him. Now he had the regime that suited him perfectly. He had a good breakfast in the morning, a packed lunch in his bag going off to college, a substantial hot dinner waiting for him when he returned in the evening. He had his own bedroom. And then he had Mrs McGinn, washing his clothes, fussing over him, telling him the news of the neighbourhood, anecdotes about local characters. At that time Seville Place and Sheriff Street were at the heart of the docker community, and if the people were not affluent as working class communities go, yet there was a sense of comfort and security in the air, since there was plenty of work for the men, and dockers were being paid well at that time.

Now my tiny bedsitter in Harcourt Street was the central meeting place. Aidan Hickey had taken a room downstairs no bigger than mine, but with his easel set up on the small patch of open floor, and his canvasses propped against the bed, there was barely enough room to squeeze past. So when Fred called he tapped on Aidan's door and the two of them would arrive up to me armed with the chocolate biscuits.

I was never a talker, so the conversations were mostly about art, mostly about Fred's latest passions. There were days when he talked of nothing but Renaissance sculpture, describing and analyzing, for example, every panel in Ghiberti's Baptistery Doors. Then he discovered a book called 'Chinese Theories of Art' which he probably borrowed from Murphy, and we spent nights, sometimes into the early hours, teasing out the Chinese vision. I remember one conundrum from that book that had us arguing,

Relief panel from his College of Art days

and analysing, and assessing, more than usual. It was an anecdote about two art collectors who had unerring eyes for works of art and had amassed the two best collections in the province. One of the collectors heard about a pottery vase that was about to be auctioned. He went to see it and sat for a long time admiring the graceful lines of the vase, the perfect proportions, the artistry of the decorative motif, the exquisite glaze. The more he looked at it, the more he was convinced that he was looking at a perfect work of art. And he was determined to purchase it. But far from being elated by its perfection he was oppressed by it. And after much consideration he decided that if he should succeed in buying it, he would knock a chip out of it, and he picked the spot on which he would inflict the damage. At the auction he was dismayed to see his rival, who proceeded to bid against him for the vase. The bids went higher and higher until eventually the price exceeded the resources of the collector and he had to concede to his rival. During the following days the collector brooded on his failure, and continued to be obsessed by the perfection of the vase. Eventually he decided to call on his rival and to tell him of his idea for improving it by damaging it. Having congratulated him on his successful purchase he asked his rival if he could see the vase again. When the vase was brought in and placed before him, he could scarcely credit his eyesight: there, exactly where he himself had intended it, was a missing chip.

Aidan was going through his Ferdinand Leger period, inspired by both the art and the political ideas of the great French painter. Fred did not share our left wing views and had little enthusiasm for politics of any shade. Aidan and I had joined the local branch of the Labour Party, and when we were alone we discussed politics non-stop. But when Fred was around any attempt to debate a political or social issue quickly foundered, and the conversation quickly veered back to an impassioned discussion of art or culture generally.

The seminar on Art and Philosophy was above my head. I knew little about art except for what I was learning from the discussions with Fred and our circle of friends. I knew less about philosophy, and the Opus Dei people were dedicated students of Thomas Aquinas. So, even though the seminar was to explore different philosophical attitudes to art, there was a smugness about them, a sense that, when all was said and done, they had their pre-packaged arguments to refute all philosophical stances that conflicted with Thomism. Donal was bright and well-read and articulate, and

Naomh Bríd. A wood carving from his College of Art days. When he returned to teach there he had specific responsibility for Wood Carving. (Now in St. Brigid's Secondary School in Tuam, Co Galway)

was able to engage with them. Henry too, in his more truncated style. Fred's contributions were passionately intense but erratic, generally not in line with the sequence of argument being pursued, but providing a colourful digression for a while, until the philosophers nudged back the discussion to the path they were following. After a few sessions I became embarrassed by my own eternal silence, and dropped out.

I enrolled in evening lectures for the BA degree at UCD. It was convenient, lectures were held in the Earlsfort Terrace centre, around the corner from my bed-sitter in Harcourt Street. It was also a curious arrangement, hundreds of students coming into the old Physics Theatre for lectures. And the only bureaucratic engagement you had with the college, once you had signed on and paid your fees, was to take examinations at the end of First Year and finally at the end of Third Year. It was the opposite of the College of Art, where they were working under supervision every day from nine in the morning to nine at night. But for me the lectures were a futile exercise: so many people packed into the one theatre created a warm heavy atmosphere, and, after my day's work in the Civil Service, I promptly fell asleep.

One evening while I was winding my way through the maze of sheds and pre-fabricated classrooms at the back of the College, I met Fred.

"What are you doing around here? This isn't your territory."

"I'm going to a lecture. Do you want to come?"

"I'm supposed to be at a lecture too, Macro-economics. What's your one?"

"Françoise Henry is giving a series of lectures on Early Christian Art in Ireland. The Purser Griffith lectures. They're free and open. Anyone can go."

"It sounds better than Macro-economics. I'll go."

So we made our way to one of the shed-like lecture rooms they called studios and sat in with thirty or forty others. Presently a plump lady took her place on the podium, and introduced herself as Professor Françoise Henry in a heavy French accent. She was going to give a series of four lectures on the development of stone sculpture in Ireland from the earliest days to the 11th century.

She turned down the lights and turned on a slide projector. Image followed image on the screen, while Françoise Henry's comments on each in her expressionless school-mistress drawl ran into a narrative, the story of how some crudely hewn motifs on megalithic stones developed into the

free-running ornamentation on the La Tène style stones, how the cross and circle symbols of the sun metamorphosed into Christian crosses and finally into the highly distinctive Irish High Crosses.

What most fascinated me was that these ornamental stones in the photographic slides were located in fields around the countryside. These were masterpieces of sculpture, thousands of years old, and they were standing casually in bogs, on top of hills, in islands, everywhere and anywhere, scattered all over the country. It was as if the whole countryside was one vast art gallery. And it was all encapsulated for me in the image of the Turoe Stone standing in a field in Co. Galway.

Fred was totally elated when we emerged from the lecture. He too had been amazed, smitten. The delicacy of the free-flowing lines on the Turoe Stone had taken his breath too. The emergence of Christian symbols directly from the Pre-Christian motifs had set his brain on fire. But, as with

Job done!
Fred inside his sculpture, Caiseal Óir, in Bunratty, Co Clare, inspired by the fibula of Celtic art

me, what most impressed him was the sense of all these monuments being part of a landscape, indeed emerging from the same landscape, expressing the character and the culture of the people who ploughed that landscape, representing their most deeply held beliefs, celebrating their sense of awe at the mystery of life and nature.

We returned to Harcourt Street, picked up the packet of milkchoc gold-grain from the little shop in the lane behind the house, and drank mug after mug of coffee while we re-visited each piece of sculpture in each site, resolving to go and see each one of them in location as soon as we possibly could.

"Are you coming to the rest of the lectures?" Fred asked as he was departing.

"What about my Macro-economics? It's on at the same time."

"Shag the economics. Economics are not important. Art is the only thing that counts when all is said and done."

"It was more interesting anyway. I would have slept through the Macro-economics, and been none the wiser. Yeah, I'll go along next Tuesday."

Another evening Fred arrived up to my bedsitter, breathless with excitement. He had two books under his arm.

"Did you ever hear of the Golden Ratio?" he asked.

"Yeah, I did it in Maths for my Leaving Cert," I replied. "Dividing a line in such a way that the small section had the same ratio to the big section as the big section had to the whole line. Is that it?"

"That's it, but it applies to all kinds of figures too, rectangles for example."

"Didn't Pythagoras build a religion around it?" I was trying to dredge up what I could recall, but mathematics was never one of my interests.

"He did. He was able to relate it to music and art as well. But the most amazing thing is that it relates to the scale of the human body."

"Which human body?" I joked.

But there was no joking with Fred when he was in full flight. He put the two books on the table, and opened one of them, Leonardo da Vinci's 'Notebooks'. He thumbed through it until he found the sketch of Vitruvius's man. Then he launched into an explanation of Leonardo's proportions of the body, that a standard male body with arms stretched out horizontally and feet together can fit into a square. When the feet are extended and the hands raised to be level with the top of the head, the body fits into a circle, the central point of which is the navel.

"What if a person has short legs and long arms?" I asked.

"That's irrelevant. What we are looking at here is a concept of beauty. What appears as beautiful to the eye has an inherent harmony, and that harmony is based on proportion, the proportion of parts to each other and parts to the whole. The Greeks understood it as the Golden Ratio and applied it to sculpture, and architecture, to painting and music. Leonardo discovered it from Vitruvius when his book on architecture was discovered and published, and it influenced Renaissance sculpture and architecture as well."

"Do you mean they had a formula?"

"It's not as simple as that. They had an ideal of beauty and what they created as beautiful in sculpture and architecture, or whatever, reflected the proportions of the ideal human body, and what they saw as beautiful in the human body reflected the same harmony that they found in art and nature. Underpinning it all was this Golden Ratio."

"It does give an insight into Greek art, maybe Renaissance sculpture too, but I can't imagine it applying to, say, Breughel. I can't imagine his figures fitting into circles and squares. And yet they are beautiful too."

"It's the harmony of the parts and the whole that counts. Here's a man who has developed that concept for the modern world." He pushed the second book towards me, Le Corbusier's 'Modular'. "He's an architect, and he has developed the concept of using the proportions of the human body as a basis for design in architecture. But he also applies it to design in every field. He even creates furniture based on the same proportions. His idea is that a more human environment can be created by adopting this scheme of human proportions."

"Mighty. Where did you get the books?"

"I borrowed them from the library in the College. Murphy was telling us about the Modular, and mentioned the books, so I got to the library first."

By then I had boiled the kettle and made two mugs of coffee.

"Have you no chocolate biscuits?" he asked.

"No, it's nearly the end of the month and I'm broke."

"I know where we'll get some. Did you ever hear of the Réalt?"

"No".

"It's the Irish-speaking branch of the Legion of Mary. They have a base up the street here and are open most nights."

"Where did you hear of them?"

"I was at a choir recital down in Conradh na Gaeilge. *Claisceadal Cois Life,* they call it. They sing songs in Irish and they're brilliant, so they were inviting me to go to the Réalt. They have a bit of singing there too."

"You must be desperate for your chocolate biscuits."

"Ah, it might be a bit of craic, and it's free."

We went. There was no singing, just talk about religion, and all they had was Marietta biscuits.

Fred's love affair with Renaissance sculpture had begun. Every time he called up to me, he had another book with him to illustrate a new discovery, from Ghiberti's Baptistery Doors to Donatello's David to Michelangelo's Moses. Always he was looking for the hidden geometry, the harmony of forms that manifested the underlying Golden Ratio.

Murphy was certainly stimulating Fred's mind, but he had a somewhat similar effect on others from our circle. Henry and Aidan, being free to pick and choose, went to his drawing classes, because they found them far superior to those in the painting department. Unlike Fred, they were uncomfortable with his greener than green nationalism and his devotion to Catholicism and to the Church. But they appreciated his provocative humour, his drawing skills, and his gifted teaching ability.

I had taken to spending evenings in the National Library. The wonderful reading room was far more pleasant than the crowded lecture halls of UCD. The Library stayed open almost to ten o'clock. One night when I came out I found Fred outside on the steps, under the pillars, locked in argument with our usual circle of friends. It was an argument that had started in Murphy's drawing class and had continued on outside. In those days, of course, the College of Art was sandwiched between the National Library and Leinster House, and it closed at nine. So here they were an hour later, with horns still locked.

Apparently Murphy had dismissed Henry Moore as second rate, and added that the English had no feeling for visual art, no sense of the aesthetic in painting or sculpture. Someone, I'm sure it was Henry Sharpe, challenged him on that, and the argument began. As usual, Henry and Aidan were in the life-drawing class of the Sculpture Department. Denis Bannister, another close friend, who hadn't been present because, as a diploma student, he did his drawing in the Painting Department, was claiming that Murphy must have been pulling their legs as he was an ardent admirer of Moore and showed Moore's influence in his own drawings which, everyone agreed, were excellent.

I don't know how Murphy fared in the argument, but here was Fred gamely defending his assertion, with passionate comparisons to Rodin and Maillol. If they were first rate then Moore was second rate.

The contradictions and objections were flying at him hot and heavy. What about Moore's sense of the monumental – just as achieved as in classical sculpture? What about Moore's exploration of the void, the relationship between the mass and the space in his bronzes?

Fred was holding his ground, not so much by faulting Moore as by extolling the superiority of Rodin and Maillol.

The argument was not resolved and nobody surrendered an inch, but they eventually ran out of steam and decided it was time to retire to the Coffee Inn. While we nursed the cups of steaming coffee that the dour Antonio placed before us, I asked them what they thought of Denis's theory that Murphy was taking the piss, that he was saying something outlandish just to provoke an argument, and, if so, hadn't he succeeded?

Fred studied pottery under Peter Brennan. When he finished in the College of Art, he presented a set of bowls he had made to his benefactor, Tom Mac Evilly, the former CEO of Co Sligo VEC. This surviving bowl is owned by Tom's daughter Geraldine Conway

They thought about it for a moment, and then turned to Fred. He was the one who knew Murphy best. Fred's opinion was that, no, Murphy was serious.

But a few days later I met Henry and asked him if Moore's place in the artistic firmament had been decided. He laughed. When they again met Murphy they tried to resurrect the subject, but he clearly wanted to move on. He said that he had had another look at Moore's work and thought that perhaps he had some merit after all, but then, he added with a wry smile, he had discovered that Moore was descended from the Irish famine emigrants. "And so," said Henry, "there is a good possibility that he was sending us all up."

All I could think was: what a teacher!

The years rolled past. Among his accolades, Fred won the prestigious Taylor Scholarship. As they completed their courses in the College, Fred, Aidan, and Henry took the direct route towards teaching. The route itself was anything but direct. In order to be fully qualified one had to have the Art Teachers' Certificate, but that involved passing what seemed like a myriad of examinations, doing modules in all sorts of crafts, clocking up teaching experience. To an outside observer it appeared like a maze they had to negotiate, with obstacles to be overcome around every corner. Many practising art teachers were working for years without the full qualifications and of course were not being paid a proper salary as a result.

However, Fred was pragmatic and sensible. He knew he had to earn his living and that art would not provide it directly, at least in the short term. He identified what he had to do, took the exams, and the modules, and the craft courses. He passed the exams with honours and took first place in Pictorial Composition, for which he was awarded a gold medal. He clocked up his teaching practice in various schools, particularly St Paul's in Raheny. And in September, 1967, he was given a full-time job by Co Meath Vocational Education Committee teaching in Navan.

Fred spent a year and a half working in Navan and was very happy there. He made friends, as he always did, and threw himself fervently into the task of turning out little Michelangelos, and raising the level of art appreciation in Meath to Medici standards. Occasionally he came to Dublin and reported on progress.

However, he wasn't long enough in Navan to create the Meath Renaissance or to become disillusioned. Half way through his second year events took over. Domhnall Ó Murchadha had moved up to the post of

Professor of Sculpture, and he was anxious to have Fred as his Assistant Professor, in other words in his own old post. No matter how happy Fred was in Navan, no matter how committed to the Vocational School there, this was an opportunity he could not ignore.

The prospect of teaming up with Murphy again obviously appealed to him. The opportunity of teaching students who were talented and dedicated to art attracted him. He also felt it would be a chance to shake up the higher echelons of the establishment in the College. They were not like Fred, nor like Murphy for that matter. They were generally academicians, who treated their College commitments as subsidiary to everything

Thomas Ashe Memorial, Dingle, Co Kerry. Fred's first commissioned sculpture

else in their careers and ran it as a late Victorian institution. However, by the sixties change was in the air, new approaches were being adopted in the art world elsewhere, but these people were too set in their ways to adapt and to forge a new identity for the college, so the overall atmosphere was one of uncertainty, even of paralysis. But it was a challenge that Fred relished, and he applied for the job, even though he would be giving up a full-time permanent post with an annual salary and returning to part-time status and being paid by the hour.

Of course he got the job, and in February, 1969, Fred returned to Dublin. As it happened I was on the lookout for a flat at the time and so we rented one in Kilmainham and shared it until the summer, the only time we lived under the one roof in all our years in Dublin.

Those few months were certainly eventful. I was teaching in Clondalkin and was heavily involved in Labour politics. There was an election that year. Fred threw himself into his teaching with his characteristic energy and enthusiasm. We had just settled into our different grooves when we went to a dance on the night of the 1st of March. Dances were still the main arena where boys met girls. We went to the Television Club back on our old stomping ground of Harcourt Street. That was the night Fred met Kathleen McGreal, whom he was to marry three years later. From that night on, Kathleen was to be his beacon, his muse, the rock to which he clung whenever he was in danger of being submerged.

So the future looked bright, looked as if it could be charted from that moment ever upwards, predictable. They were days of optimism.

But the optimism didn't last long. Almost immediately student protests began in the College of Art. It followed the historic protests in France the previous year, and protests in other Irish colleges. The list of grievances of the students was long and, for the most part, genuine. Simply they were saying that the College was being run on Victorian lines, and that the authorities were making no attempt to introduce the kind of professionalism that was expected in the dynamic 1960s. I had heard it all before, from Henry, Aidan, Denis, John, yes, and most vehemently from Fred himself.

The disturbances continued, teaching was disrupted. There was a threat of the students being locked out, then there was an occupation of the College by the students. Everything ground to a halt.

A few teachers, including Denis, openly sympathised with the student protests. A few others sympathised but kept their heads down. Most were

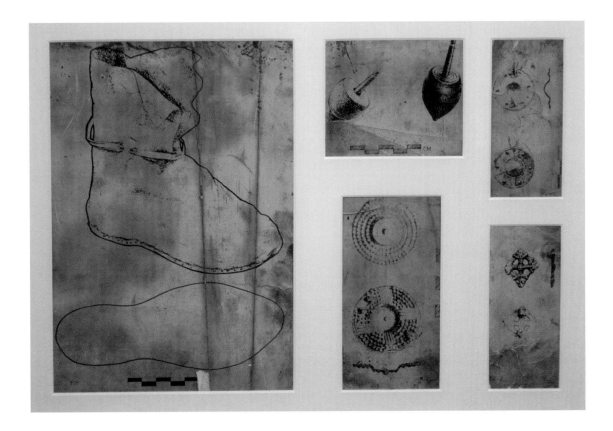

so out-of-touch with the realities of the 1960s that they didn't even grasp the issues.

Fred had just started his teaching career in the College, alive with his characteristic passion for art. He viewed the disturbances as an unwelcome distraction from what students and teachers should be focused on. The more disruptive the disturbances became, the more frustrated he became. He was also indignant that the protests were motivated by political considerations in many cases, rather than artistic or aesthetic ones. And he was totally outspoken about his frustrations. Such was his single-minded commitment to art that he felt students should put up with problems and get on with the only issue worth spending energy on.

But if Fred had given a moment's reflection even to his own conditions of employment, he might have felt the urge to join the barricades. In the whole college there were only a few professors who had full-time permanent employment. Even as Assistant Professor, Fred was employed

Sample of his drawings of some of the artefacts found in the High Street, Wood Quay, Dublin, excavations

Fred unravelling
the spiral

to teach on a part-time basis and paid by the hour for the time he spent
before a class, so many hours per week during the term. There was no
holiday pay, no guarantee of employment the following year, no pension
rights.

But Fred did not reflect on this at all. His idealism, and desire to be
immersed in art, blinkered him. He saw the protesting students as purely
interested in agitation, for the sake of agitation, following the trend of the
time for demonstrations and occupations and street protests. With the vast
majority of the staff maintaining a low profile, and Fred openly vociferous

in his condemnation of the protests, he became an easy target for the students. On one occasion a television crew from RTÉ had been spirited into the College by the students, and when they entered the Sculpture Department where Fred was teaching, he challenged them and demanded that they leave. There was a heated argument, in which he expressed himself in his usual forthright way. But he realised only afterwards that he was being filmed unawares. He issued a solicitor's letter to RTÉ who then undertook not to broadcast any of the material they had filmed. But Fred was very hurt by that incident and it triggered a rapid disillusion with the College.

Unfortunately, he also saw himself as being of a different mind to the rest of us, his close friends. Myself and Aidan were involved in left-wing politics, something he linked to the protesting students. Denis, who had also been on the staff of the College, openly stated support for the protesting students. So Fred felt more alienated than he should have.

With the total closure of the College Fred was out of work. The archaeological excavations at High Street and Winetavern Street were in full swing at the time, conducted by the National Museum. Both he and Denis had worked occasionally there on a part-time basis, primarily making drawings of all the artefacts found on the sites. Fred got some work there now to keep him going.

Fred's disillusion with the College of Art was too deep and too heartfelt to allow him resume where he left off, when it eventually re-opened and re-commenced normal business. He could no longer work up the enthusiasm he needed to teach in the only way he could. He submitted his resignation. Denis was dismissed from his post for 'disloyalty' to the College staff. He got the Union to contest this dismissal and was re-instated, but immediately submitted his resignation. So the whole episode had left a very sour legacy for everyone.

But Fred had also become deeply disillusioned with Dublin. He was still quite a devout Catholic, didn't drink, retained an idealistic attitude to women despite his exposure to the bohemian and hippy lifestyle of the art world. He had a deep longing to return to the purer world of rural Ireland, as he saw it, to the landscape of megalith, and high cross, and ancient mysteries. He longed to be back in Sligo.

He applied for a job with County Sligo VEC and was installed as a full-time teacher in Sligo town in September, 1971.

72

## Chapter 4

# The Teaching Years

Fred settled into life in Sligo in his own usual energetic way. He was happy, relatively speaking, and seemed determined to purge himself of the negative experience of his last couple of years in Dublin. And so began a period of almost two decades when work and family took over both our lives. We both got married in 1972, and ended up with five children each to rear. I continued teaching in Clondalkin where Celia and I bought a newly built house and struggled to pay the mortgage. Fred and Kathleen had their own house built on a beautiful site between Sligo and Strandhill. And of course they too had the mortgage to pay at punitive rates, like everyone else.

At first we were able to keep up contact with regular visits, but the arrival of children began to slow us down, until eventually we saw each other as rarely as once or twice a year, and even then it was with children in tow.

But, Fred being the lively passionate talker, I got a briefing each time I met him on how his life was progressing. He loved being back in Sligo, loved being reintegrated into the landscape that had impressed itself on his mind and soul when he was a child. His chief pleasure was to go out to Easkey, take his fishing rod, and cast his line off the rocks down by the Cimin. He had peace there.

In September 1972, the Regional College opened in Sligo, and Fred was appointed a lecturer with the job of setting up an Art Department. This was the perfect job for him, starting from the blank page, with considerable freedom to develop art as part of this third level college. And of course he weighed in with his enormous enthusiasm.

He was a gifted teacher. His enthusiasm for his subject was enough to

*Facing page:*
Detail from
Eibhear Alban,
Shekina Garden,
Co Wicklow

73

guarantee success. But Fred had much more than that. He had a deep interest in people, and so he related to his students on the basis of their being of central and prime importance. He searched for whatever talent he could find in them, and then encouraged them to build on that talent. He was never blinded by his own lofty vision of art; in teaching he was able to look sympathetically at what his students were struggling to achieve, and to rejoice in their usually moderate success.

The Art Department flourished, and after the Preliminary Course was complete with the first batch of students, it divided into two sections, Painting and Sculpture, with Fred taking Sculpture.

But there were frustrations too. His strengths ensured that the Art Department was vibrant, the teaching exciting, and the students motivated and enthusiastic. However, his weaknesses did not go away. Fred wanted Art to be the crown jewel of the College, central to its activity and identity. But this was a college of technology, set up to provide an advanced education in the areas of Science, Business, Engineering, as well as Art. And

Wedding photo.
*Left to right:* Pat, Mary (his sister), Fred, Kathleen, Bridie, Nora, and the flower girl is Mary's daughter Angela Eggleston

all the emphasis in the country at the time was for these colleges to serve industrial and business needs.

There were times when Fred felt that the Art Department was not getting parity of esteem with the other departments, in terms of budget for example. And one time I remember him being furious about the allocation of space. His Sculpture section was being allocated space at a first floor level, despite his protestations that this would preclude students from working with stone to any serious extent – you can't drive a fork-lift up the stairs!

True to his nature, Fred was utterly incapable of achieving his goals by subtle means, compromising here, cajoling there, massaging egos somewhere else. No, like the heroes of Shakespearean tragedy, his strength was his weakness. What made him exceptional with a chisel in his hand, or in front of a class, brought him into head-butting confrontations with people who saw their priorities as other than the pursuit of beauty.

One hilarious example was when he appeared before an interview board for promotion. The scenario was that as the College grew and departments within it grew, higher grade lecturing posts were created. In the normal course of events, those who were in the departments and were performing successfully would be automatic choices for upgrading. But procedures had to be followed: posts had to be advertised, interviews held, and applicants appointed in a transparent and accountable manner. In this way, the position of Head of Sculpture was being upgraded, the post was advertised, and interviews were being held. There could have been no greater certainty than that Fred would get the higher post. It was a rubber stamp job. No doubt there were other horses in the field but none of them at the races.

So Fred goes in to the Interview Board, the Chairperson greets him in the routine way and proceeds to introduce the other members of the Board. When he introduces one member as an Inspector from the Department of Education, Fred queries, "but you're not one of the Art Inspectors?" He replies, "no, I'm an inspector of – whatever subject." "So, how are you qualified to sit on this board, then?" Fred asks. "I'm qualified because I am an Inspector of the Department of Education, and I'm here to ensure the procedures of the Department are adhered to." "And is this the attitude of the Department to Art, that any old inspector will do, that they don't need to send someone who knows something about the subject?" And so on, and so on.

Getting away from it all. Fred shore-fishing off the pier in Easkey

I don't know if there was any semblance of a normal interview after that, but the mayhem created by Fred ensured that the Board made no appointment. He was fortunate that his achievements were so good, and his standing so high with the other members of the Board that they would not countenance appointing someone else over his head. Understandably, the Inspector would not countenance appointing Fred on the basis of that interview. The stalemate was eventually resolved by the College re-advertising the post. And the next time Fred went into the interview with the expletive-laden admonitions of his friends and his suffering wife ringing in his ears to keep his mouth under control. He did, and he was duly appointed.

Fred and Kathleen had five children, Orla, Elaine, Niall, Pauric, and Finn, born between 1973 and 1981. Kathleen was a primary school teacher, so the logistics of managing such a large family were challenging, to put it mildly. Fred was a dedicated, passionately loving, husband and father in the traditional mould. He had not the slightest inclination towards bohemian laissez-faire, so the Conlon children were ferried to their music classes and their swimming, and brought up just like other children.

What was Fred like in the family context? As I have said, this was the period when I had least contact with him, so I cannot claim to have witnessed much of the family dynamic at first hand. But I gather that, as in every other aspect of his life, Fred had his strengths, and sometimes his strengths misapplied. He was ambitious for his children, his goals were high, and he himself was prepared to move mountains to help them achieve their goals. But children become teenagers, and sometimes the last thing they want is the enthusiastic involvement of their parents in their lives. All his children worshipped him, he was that kind of person, apart from being that type of father. But Niall, in particular, inherited some of Fred's stubborn streak and, as a result, their relationship was turbulent. It fell to Kathleen to keep the peace, and to keep the family sailing on an even keel, something she did with total competence.

Another problem was that Fred in his way was as needy and demanding of support as any of the children. He had no ego whatsoever, and there was never the slightest posturing of the artist demanding indulgence and pampering because of his personal importance. Fred never saw himself as important, but he attached enormous importance to whatever he was doing at the time, talked about it, involved everyone in it, and needed to have life organised for him so that he could achieve it. This characteristic

also put huge strains on family life. His enthusiasm was so infectious, his sincerity so pure that those around him made enormous concessions to his needs. Of course Kathleen was permanently in the eye of the storm, the calm centre around which the vortex of Fred's turbulent activity circled interminably.

Fred had very talented students in due course who attest to his inspirational teaching, such as Jackie McKenna and Eileen McDonagh. Eileen was attracted to sculpture by Fred's zeal and his skill both as teacher and artist. She studied under him from 1975 to 1978, and subsequently became a close friend and colleague. When she and another student displayed an interest in stone, and there was inadequate facility for stone work in the college, due probably to the afore-mentioned first-floor location, Fred brought them out to his own studio beside his house. He set

At home in Tully, Fred and Kathleen with their children. Finn on Kathleen's knee. The others from left, Elaine, Pauric, Niall and Orla

them up to work there, giving them the benefit of his private tuition.

What fascinated Eileen then, and still does to this day, was Fred's absolute facility in every medium, drawing, clay modelling, wood-carving, stone-carving, etc etc, and his absolute control of every instrument he took in his hand, from a pencil to a chisel.

Fred derived great satisfaction from his teaching, and from the success of his students, especially the success of students like Eileen and Jackie who went on to scale the heights of sculpture. He also had the satisfaction of seeing his family growing up in a happy, secure, and comfortable home environment. He was being treated with great respect in Sligo on the basis of his reputation as an extraordinary teacher. But behind all of this, throughout his teaching years, there was a deep and fundamental frustration, a growing unhappiness that devoured any sense of satisfaction or feelings of self-worth.

The nub of the problem was that, throughout his teaching years, Fred had produced very little work of his own. Yes, as close to nothing as makes no difference. His token output of finished pieces from 1971 to 1989, amounted to no more than one or two every year, just enough to demonstrate his talent and remind himself and those around him of the enormous potential he was neglecting.

Fred could not compartmentalise himself or his mind, could not divide himself up as a father, a teacher, an artist, could not switch from one function to the other. Neither could he coordinate all three functions simultaneously. If, for example, he was in socialising mode, and was in the company of friends, he would immerse himself totally in the demands of that moment, would forget about his stresses and responsibilities, would forget promises to be somewhere else. His mind worked only in terms of total concentration on the moment or the business in hand.

So, while he was teaching, he concentrated on it totally, almost to the level of obsession. He poured all his thoughts and ideas, and creativity into teaching. It was the focus of his mind. It was the preoccupation of his waking life. It was the overwhelming topic of his conversation. He believed in the value of what he was doing and in the benefit to his students.

But there was the problem that he was fundamentally an artist, that his most important obligation in life was to produce art. Murphy had one time advised him, in jest or in earnest, or in ironic both, that he should never marry or take on family responsibility, so that he could dedicate himself totally to art and become a truly great artist. But Fred could never have lived or functioned as such an isolated and independent figure. He needed the security and fulfilment and framework of support that only a family could provide. So he married, and had five children, and needed the job to provide for them.

There were many incidental aspects of his life and work in the Regional College that he enjoyed enormously. He made very good friends, not just in the Art Department but right across the spectrum of the College. One of the highlights of his teaching years was the annual camping holiday in France and Spain. This was a family holiday; Fred and Kathleen packed the five children into the car, the trailer with tent hitched behind. They almost always went in tandem with Andy and Bernie Moynihan and their four children. Andy was a colleague of Fred's in the Regional College. And of course the itinerary was designed to accommodate visits to old churches, cathedrals, art galleries, and other places on Fred's hit-list. Andy, who was a scientist, often joked about his growing knowledge of Romanesque architecture and medieval sculpture. These holidays during which he was able to acquaint himself first-hand with the art and culture of France and Spain helped to sustain Fred over these years and to keep his inspiration and desire sharp.

However, as the years were passing, the niggling gnawing discontent grew. His life was passing and he was aware of the work he might have been doing, the ideas he might have been exploring in stone or wood or bronze. He never begrudged his students the benefit of his teaching, but the awareness that he was pouring his creativity into their lives and their work began to undermine even the satisfaction he had been getting from teaching. Because his nature was fundamentally generous he did not become bitter or cynical. Instead he became angry. And this anger born of frustration grew steadily over the years. By the mid-eighties his existence was hell and he wanted to get out of teaching altogether. But he had a family to support, so this was not an option. And I suspect he must have been very difficult to live with in these years.

Then in 1989 the golden opportunity dropped from on high. The state at this time was almost bankrupt. It was the time when citizens were asked to tighten their belts, to do without, to pay more taxes, and to be satisfied with a more meagre public service. Jobs were being shed everywhere, recruitment became an historical concept, rationalisation became a national preoccupation. When the budget for education was cut, schools and colleges had to 'rationalise'. That meant providing the same service with fewer staff. Sligo Regional College was affected like every other institution dependent on the public purse. And the debate on 'rationalisation' began. Amalgamation of courses and subjects and departments was seen as a way to economise on staff. Redundancies and early retirements were on offer to achieve this 'downsizing'.

In all this flux of rationalisation, Fred saw his opportunity. Early retirement with a small pension entered the realm of possibility. He had over twenty years of teaching service behind him, and there was a bonus of a few years on offer as part of the state's redundancy scheme. It would be a long way short of the income he had. And the financial needs of his growing family were going to be greater rather than less in the immediate future. University fees were still in place, a looming cloud on the horizon of any family with aspirations to a third level education.

He discussed it – I would imagine long and intensely – with Kathleen. In the usual pattern it would be she, the mother, who would be contemplating giving up the full time job. And it was not as if a freed-up Fred would account for the logistical needs of the family. If he were to take responsibility for getting the children up and out in the morning, collecting them and driving them hither and thither in the afternoon, cooking the dinner in the evening, supervising their homework at night, he would no doubt still have a nil output and his anger would be directed at his family.

Kathleen's devotion to Fred as a person and her belief in him as an artist were absolute. She was clear-headed about his shortcomings too. She agreed to continue in her teaching job, while he could apply for early retirement. The one condition was that he would devote his whole time and energy to sculpture and endeavour to supplement his pension with earnings from his art.

He applied for the redundancy package on offer and was granted it. In 1989 he left teaching and became a full-time artist for the first time in his life.

# Chapter 5

# The Years of Artistic Output

During the late eighties when Fred was agonising over his teaching career and his decision to retire, I was heavily involved in my own issues. Apart from family commitments, I was now Principal of a large school, Lucan Community College, and that made considerable demands on my time and energy. Over and above that, I had embarked on a project to set up the Irish Writer's Union and the Irish Writer's Centre. So whenever I met Fred, we were briefing each other on what was happening, rather than being actively involved in each other's life.

Once he retired in 1989, there was a total change in Fred. The shackles were off, he was free to be a full-time artist, and he bounded into his new life with zeal and energy. He whose output had been miniscule over the previous twenty years exploded into creativity.

But miniscule as his output had been previously, there were elements there which provided the springboard for his successes from 1989 onwards.

In his retreat to Sligo in 1971 Fred put distance between himself and his experience of the previous two years in Dublin. But he also distanced himself from everything that was happening in art circles. His occasional exhibit at the Oireachtas or other art exhibitions always attracted attention, often won an award, but it still did not integrate him in any significant way into the art community of Dublin.

*Facing page:*
Detail from
Casadh Na
Gealaí, Rosses
Point, Co Sligo

Two of his most outstanding students, Eileen McDonagh and Jackie McKenna, recognised this alienation, and when they left the college and moved into their own careers as sculptors they nudged Fred into an involvement he did not have before. And there were things happening. The Sculptors' Society had been set up and was lobbying for more commissions for sculptors. It was also providing information to practitioners on opportunities that were arising. But the most significant development, in so far as it influenced Fred, was the initiation of Sculpture Symposia.

He participated in his first Symposium, in Barr na Coille where there were two granite quarries in the Dublin mountains, in 1984. A sculpture symposium was a straightforward concept. A sponsor invited a number of sculptors to work in a specific location for a set period of time. The sponsor provided the material and support services. Sometimes the sculptors were paid a stipend as well as a living allowance and the finished pieces were donated to the sponsor for exhibition in situ. Sometimes the sponsor provided less support, but the sculptors retained ownership of the pieces they produced. Either way, there was an exciting dynamic generated by having the artists work in close proximity, exchanging ideas, providing mutual encouragement and a sense of community or common cause.

The Symposium in Barr na Coille fired Fred with enthusiasm. He had a long-standing link with the granite quarries in the Dublin mountains going back to his time as a student when he accompanied Domhnall Ó Murchadha to collect stone for his various commissions. Also, Paddy Roe, who belonged to one of the quarrying families, was a fellow-student of Fred's and became a close friend. Fred would often wax eloquent about the distinct traditions and culture among the families that had worked these stone quarries in the Dublin mountains for many generations. So, this Symposium could not have been located in a more amenable or inspirational place. The participants, twelve Irish and two foreign invitees, included Eileen McDonagh, Cliodhna Cussen, Jackie McKenna, and Noel Hoare, and were all people whom Fred related to positively. They were all congenial company, stimulating minds, and accomplished artists. So, the experience of working alongside them for that summer of 1984, was healing as well as inspiring. It was a blistering hot summer and the lunch breaks in the shade provided the opportunity of long and deep discussions that were resumed in the evenings in the local house that had been rented to accommodate the foreign visitors.

Casadh Na
Gealaí, where it
was sculpted at
the Symposium
in Barr na Coille

Fred produced the abstract garden piece, called 'Casadh na Gealaí', which was subsequently bought by the collector Vincent Ferguson and his wife, Noleen, and sited at Rosses Point, across the bay from Fred's house. Even as he was working on it in the Dublin mountains, he was drawing his inspiration from the Sligo landscape.

In the following year, the summer of 1985, there was another Symposium, sponsored among others by the Sculptors' Society, County Sligo VEC, and Coillte – the state agency for forests – and it was right on Fred's doorstep in Hazelwood, the beautiful wooded shore of Lough Gill, just outside Sligo town. Many of the participating sculptors were former students of Fred's from the Regional College. The sponsors wanted to install a sculpture trail along the shore of the lake to provide an additional walkway attraction for visitors. This time the material was wood, provided by Coillte, and the concept was to locate the wood sculptures back in their natural environment. It was one of the first attempts to provide site-specific pieces designed to remain in situ and it was highly successful. The pieces varied from the monumental warrior with horse and chariot completed by James McKenna, but not within the specified time, and Fred's delicate 'Sos Sliabh an Dá Éan'.

Fred wanted to create an image for restful meditation. If we examine the pattern and significance of his symbolism in this piece we will understand better how his mind worked in producing later and more important pieces. Fred was most at ease doing site-specific sculpture. His relating the design to the locale was not a sop to the sponsor or commissioner: place inspired him. His own place, Co Sligo, was an ongoing ever-present source of spiritual sustenance. But Fred saw the sacredness of other places also, and other people's places; he approached a location with reverence when called on to site a sculpture in it. Lough Gill is set in one of the most beautiful landscapes one could imagine. That landscape being Co Sligo made it so much more significant for Fred. The site he was allocated for his piece was right on the shore, facing out on to the lake and its array of islands. On the other side of the lake was Sliabh Daeane, so called in Irish because in profile it resembled two birds perched at rest. So, he took that profile and replicated it in his sculpture. However, Fred's attitude to nature then came into play. It was more than that of a sightseer, it was deep and reverential. So the image he created is also suggestive of the Tau Cross, an old sun symbol subsequently adopted by the Christian Church, in particular by St Francis, who worshipped with outstretched arms, often, we are told,

until the birds came and perched on them. So, with this mixture of Pagan and Christian symbolism, Fred created an image suggesting the ecstatic worship of the beauty of nature.

The sculpture trail consisted entirely of wood pieces, and alas, because of lack of care and maintenance, the entire collection has succumbed to erosion by the weather and the depredation of vandals. It no longer exists.

The next Sculpture Symposium that Fred attended was in Kildrummy, Aberdeenshire, Scotland, in the summer of 1987. They were working with granite, and Fred produced the stunning 'Eibhear Alban', which now stands in the Shekina Sculpture Garden in Co. Wicklow. It was his first exploration of the Spiral motif of which I have spoken in the introductory chapter.

In the summer of 1989, immediately after his retirement, Fred was given the assignment of directing a similar project, to celebrate the 50th anniversary of the death of Sligo's most famous son, William Butler Yeats. The Yeats Workshop was run on Symposium lines but with more international than national artists. It was coordinated by the Sligo Art Gallery, located in the Yeats Memorial Building, and ironically the Administrator of the Gallery

Sos Sliabh Dá Éan, looking across Lough Gill, Co Sligo

87

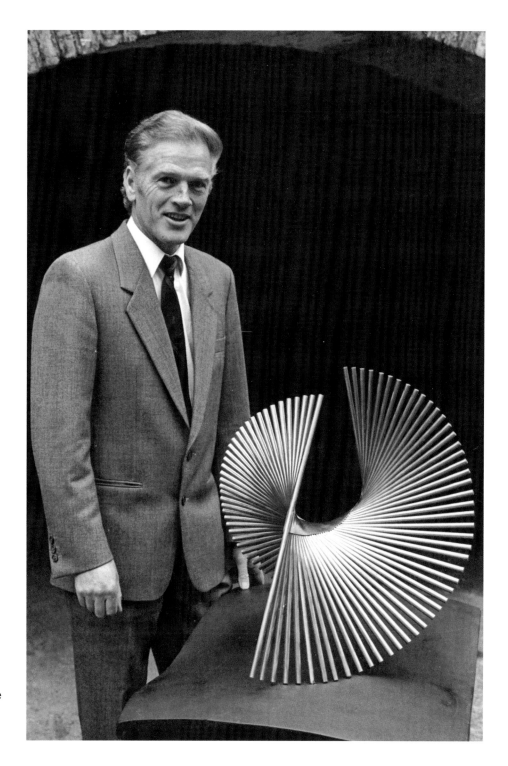

Fred posing with the model he submitted for the Dublin Airport Roundabout was Ronan Mac Evilly, son of Tom Mac Evilly, the former CEO of Co Sligo VEC, who had been instrumental in securing the scholarship for Fred to attend the College of Art back in 1961.

So, even though he had been producing only an occasional piece during his later teaching years, Fred was establishing footholds so that when he retired from teaching, he had some calling cards, and doors to knock on.

He was remarkably successful over the next few years in securing commissions. Thanks mainly to the Sculptors' Society, procedures had been established for the advertising and specification of commissions and for the assessment of applications. Of course there were many commissions he failed to get. One, which he would have dearly loved, was a monument to the poet WB Yeats, in Sligo town. Another was for a piece on the roundabout at the entrance to Dublin Airport – in this case he was short-listed, and his model was shown at an exhibition in the ILAC Centre.

One of the first commissions he did secure was for a piece outside the Library in Roscommon town. Ironically, it was across the road from the Christian Brothers' School I attended to do my Leaving Certificate. The Library had been a frequent refuge of mine. On Wednesday afternoons my class trooped up to the playing field for Gaelic Football. More often than not I dodged into the Library to spend a more pleasant and productive afternoon. So I was delighted when Fred's sculpture was sited near the front gate. It was another variation on the spiral theme.

In 1991 Fred attended another Sculpture Symposium, this time an international one, in Cochin, in the state of Kerala, India. He was very excited by what he saw of Indian culture. Its deep-rooted traditions and overt spirituality appealed to him and he looked for bonds with Irish culture. The piece he produced for the Subhash Bose Park was a meditation piece which combined Indian and Irish images. At the centre was another Spiral sculpture, surrounded by a circle of water, surrounded again by a circular band with counterbalancing expanding and contracting black and white strips of shingle.

The most significant commission that Fred received at this time was for a bronze statue of Charles Stewart Parnell, to be erected in the Parnell National Park in Rathdrum, Co. Wicklow, not far from the statesman's home in Avondale, on the centenary of his death, 1991. Modelling this figure, 8 foot 4 inches tall, in clay in his own studio was a challenge, but what a challenge. Even though the image was already determined, a life-like presentation of the statesman, Fred nevertheless contemplated and studied the setting. His figure of Parnell relates to, even grows out of, the landscape. He presents him as he would have been in that setting, among people and views that he loved, looking towards Avondale in the distance, comfortable, relaxed, and yet every inch the uncrowned king of Ireland.

The Parnell statue made a huge impression and quickly became a focal point and an attraction for the town of Rathdrum. Fred's meticulous research of the locality in the process of getting a sense of the place also made a big impression on the people. And seven years later, when they were commissioning a monument to the 1798 Rebellion they awarded it to him. After his death they erected a memorial stone to celebrate his work on their two monuments, and it was unveiled by Kathleen in the presence of the family.

He had scarcely finished the Parnell statue when he got another very large commission, a stone sculpture for a roadside location outside Bunratty Castle in Co Clare. There was a substantial budget for this work, and the location, so close to the castle, Fred decided, required a piece on a grand scale. His sense of the sacredness of place again brought him delving into the history and traditions and culture of the locality. As I have explained, his sculptures were site specific, but this clinical term does not describe the way Fred wanted his works to grow out of the earth in which they were situated, like an oak tree, like a high cross, like one of the decorated ritual stones that marked out a location of worship for our Neolithic ancestors. So the nearby mound for the inauguration of the Kings of Thomond, and the hoard of gold ornaments from the Celtic era discovered locally, all impressed on his imagination and emerged in the monumental fibula, the largest stone sculpture executed in Ireland in a century. And of course Fred never wanted his sculptures to be merely admired from a distance, he wanted people to approach, to enter breathlessly as if entering the cleft in the Split Rock, to feel and enjoy the texture of it, to use it as an amenity. Hence the inside of the fibula can seat a small community, a group of children, workers on their lunch break, and Fred loved to see his sculpture taken to the hearts of the local people in this way.

Another commission for a very different community and a very different location brought Fred right back to the area of Dublin where he spent so many years while in the College of Art. Not far from the little alleys off

Seville Place where he watched the children playing street games, he was executing a bronze sculpture for Dublin City Council at a little housing development in Portland Row. And it was the children's street games that inspired this piece, entitled 'Beds'.

By 1995 the stream of commissions inexplicably dried up. After five or six years of constant intense work, Fred found himself strangely under-pressurised, shall we say. One day he visited me in Dublin and was explaining this, and talking of embarking on a series of small works for exhibition purposes. He took out some photos of small pieces he had and we were looking through them. One of the photos caught my eye. It was of a mother and child in granite.

"That doesn't look like a small piece," I said.

He took the photo. "No," he said, "that's life-size. But the people who commissioned it reneged on the deal. They paid a deposit, but didn't come up with the rest of the money."

"Where is it now?"

"It's lying above in Paddy Roe's quarry in the Dublin Mountains."

Fred working on 'Síochán' in Cochin, India, no doubt explaining to the local artists his theory of the spiral

I took back the photo. I had fallen for this piece immediately and wanted it for my school in Lucan. "How much do you want for it?"

"Why?"

"You know my school. It would make a perfect centre-piece for the courtyard inside the front door."

"It would."

"If I could afford it."

"Well, I couldn't be too hard on you, could I?"

"That's what I'd be worried about. I won't buy it if you don't quote me a price that is reasonable for you. Work out the lowest reasonable price and then I will see if I can raise the money."

So he came back to me with a price he would be happy with. Of course it was only a fraction of what it was really worth, but money was still very scarce in 1995 and I could not use any school funds. So I went out with the begging bowl to sponsors and got a little here, a little there. Then I did a brochure for the unveiling and squeezed advertisements out of our suppliers and friendly companies. I reached the target and the sculpture was ours.

Paddy Roe and his workmen arrived with the sculpture before Fred on the day of the siting, and began to locate it on the concrete base we had put into the middle of the grass lawn of the courtyard. He asked me which way I wanted the figure faced. I thought it would be best to have the mother facing towards the front entrance. So Paddy started to work.

When Fred arrived he almost exploded.

"What are you doing?" he roared at Paddy.

"I was siting it."

"But which way are you facing it?"

"Jack said he wanted it facing this way."

"I don't give a shit which way Jack wants it faced. Look at the sun. You're facing it north."

So the two of them rapidly freed the sculpture and the plinth from the quick-drying cement and re-oriented the figure at a right angle to the one I had suggested. And of course Fred was right. The sunlight falling on the woman's face cast shadows that highlighted her features which would have been lost if her face was in shadow.

I organised an official unveiling and had Austin Currie, then a Junior Minister in Education, officiate with dignitaries like TK Whitaker present. Talking to Fred afterwards, I realised that such a total focus on the new

Working on the
Parnell statue at
his studio in Tully

work was a departure. One of the huge shortcomings of producing public sculpture associated with building projects was that the focus was on the building itself when there was an official celebration at the end. The piece of sculpture was unveiled as a by-the-way. And of course there was no critical review or notice in the newspapers. Nothing. These were the most prominent works of art throughout the country and the art critics never bothered to examine them, let alone celebrate them. And of course for the artist it was frustrating to have poured so much time and energy and thought into a work and then see it largely disregarded when it was finally sited.

The official title of the 'Mother and Child' was Iontas, (wonder). It was such a powerful symbol and representation of the loving care a parent has for a child, and which school tries to replicate, that it was taken to heart and soul by everybody, students, teachers, parents, and became the mascot and emblem of the College. Every time I stressed this to Fred, he was pleased, because above all he wanted his work to give enjoyment to ordinary people.

Even though the commissions were keeping him occupied and providing him with a livelihood, Fred retained an abiding interest in symposia. In 1996 he was back in India in Gulbarga, returning with new ideas and new techniques. But the symposium in Nanao in Japan the following year was to have an even greater influence on him.

In Japan the emphasis was on light. Of course light is a preoccupation with every artist and with every work. There are conventions, and for traditional sculpture there is the assumption of sunlight illuminating the figure from certain angles, highlighting and shadowing. But in Nanao they were playing with artificial light illuminating the forms from unexpected angles, making the light an integral part of the piece rather than something external, constant and conventional.

Even on the other side of the earth, Fred's imagination was returning to Neolithic Ireland for his inspiration. He was thinking of Newgrange and the light entering briefly at the winter solstice to illuminate the chamber deep inside the mound. So the sculpture he created had a light source in the base illuminating, from the interior, shapes and forms that were not highlighted by natural sunlight.

When he returned he was fired with enthusiasm, and itching to experiment with alternative illumination. His first opportunity was in the design of the 1798 Memorial in Rathdrum. In daylight it has a traditional tomblike appearance, four rectangular granite slabs mounted on a plinth, with flame shapes cut out of the slabs on two opposite sides and pike shapes out of the other two. But a strong interior light shines through the voids at night making these shapes visible from afar. The allusion is to the signal beacon lit by the rebels on top of hills to communicate messages.

He was to experiment again with internal lighting when I commissioned him to do a second piece for Lucan Community College. The Per Cent for Art Scheme had been introduced just as I was having an extension built to the school. Having adorned one courtyard with his 'Iontas', I wanted another piece for the other internal courtyard. The Millennium celebration was due, so we decided in the school to re-structure the second courtyard into an amenity garden for the students. And when I got the approval from the Department of Education I engaged Fred to create a Millennium Sculpture as the central feature of this garden.

Fred wanted to do an abstract piece as counterpoint to the figurative sculpture in the other courtyard. So he played around with the image of the two Millennia becoming three, and came up with two upright shafts supporting three horizontal beams. Then he wanted to integrate the concept of the third Millennium of Christianity beginning, so he introduced a light source in the base, shining through a large aperture in the first cross-beam, through a smaller one in the second cross-beam, and lighting up the underside of the third and top cross-beam. Sure enough the sculpture was transformed when the light was turned on after dark. As the school was open most nights, especially in winter, the sculpture that the evening students experienced was very different to the one the day students identified with.

When Fred got a commission from Kerry Co Council to provide a piece for the town park in Tralee, close to the Siamsa Tíre theatre, he decided on the figure of a blacksmith. Siamsa were famous for their celebration of traditional crafts and craftspeople, so it was an appropriate choice. But Fred's inspiration came from elsewhere. The crossroads, around which our houses huddled in Killeenduff, the focal point of the townland, the hub of activity, the recognised meeting place for men women and children, was called the Forge Corner. It was the site of what was called a 'smithy' on the maps for hundreds of years. And my father was the last of the blacksmiths at the Forge Corner. But when we were children the forge was vibrant, as I have indicated, the hub of local activity, the centre of communal interaction and gossip.

At the heart of this, was the blacksmith, hammering metal into shape on the anvil, pulling the iron rings red hot from the fire and banging them into place over the wooden cart wheels, nailing shoes on the hooves of the great plough-horses. It obviously left an impression on Fred too, because he called his piece 'Draíocht an Ghabha' or the magic of the blacksmith.

When he told me his thoughts on this commission, he recounted all these childhood experiences, and asked me if I had any photo of my father at work. Of course I hadn't and I was aware that none had ever been taken. But I rooted out whatever old photos I had, mostly posed shots for Communion or Confirmation occasions. They were not much use. But then there was one shot of my family with my father standing in a typical pose, as if he were about to spring into action, with his elbows out and drawn back. "That's what I remember", exclaimed Fred, "his elbows." And sure enough he was famous for his elbows. As an acclaimed Gaelic footballer he extended his sphere of influence on the pitch by means of these jostling elbows – he did not strike opponents but his elbows were there like pointed stakes in a palisade fence and opponents ran into them at their peril.

Fred was delighted with the sculpture when he had it finished, and felt that, even if he had not managed an exact likeness of my father in the features, he had certainly got a family resemblance. However, for the first time he intimated that he was struggling with the physical demands of carving such a piece and that he would probably never embark on such an undertaking again. His shoulders were reacting to the years of hammer and chisel work. Martha Quinn, who worked with him as his assistant on that sculpture, described to me how he had to support his elbows in all sorts of ways in order to use the tools. It was an impressive swan song, and poignant that it was so intimately related to our shared childhood. However, it was not totally alarming, as Fred could still work in bronze – clay modelling was not physically exacting. And in his later abstract stone pieces he could design in such a way that much of the work could be done with power-tools.

One of Fred's last commissions was from Dublin City Council for an artwork associated with a small housing project called Poddle Close, off the Clonard Road. The commission specified that the artist had to engage with the community in deciding on and designing the art work. Fred took this aspect of the commission very seriously and it threw him into confusion. He discussed it with me and asked me to come to the meetings with the local people. I suggested he not take it so seriously, that if the people were simply introduced to the creative process and shown at various stages how the work was developing, it would be an enlightening experience and they would value the finished piece all the more. But Fred couldn't see it that way and felt obliged to elicit ideas and suggestions from them. It was totally at odds with his normal approach to developing a concept. So after a couple of meetings the people, mainly the children, came up with ideas, personages associated with the area, Brendan Behan, Phil Lynott, boxers, and an image from the city centre where many of the families originated, the Pigeon House. He gave some art classes to the children and brought them to Manorhamilton to see the four plaques that they had decided on being cast. He honoured the brief he was given, but in most ways it was one of the least satisfying or satisfactory of his works.

# Chapter 6

# His Work

Fred was lucky to have had so many commissions as soon as he went full-time into sculpture. He was not an organised systematic worker by nature. He was close to the opposite. When he was working on something, he tackled it with total commitment of time, energy, and thought, spending all his waking hours on the job. Kathleen often told me of the night he had his 'eureka' moment when he was designing the piece for Bunratty Castle: he was so excited he woke her up to show her his drawing – at four in the morning! However, when he was not immediately involved in a particular project, he could sleep until lunchtime, ramble down to the shop for a packet of cigarettes and the Irish Times, and fritter away the afternoon. So the constant stream of commissions ensured that he was highly productive most of the time.

When I was raising the money to buy 'Iontas' for Lucan Community College, I produced a small brochure with biographical details and photographs of some of his previous sculptures. The purpose of it was to sell the advertising space. But Fred afterwards found the brochure extremely useful for showing to prospective clients, and he began putting together a more comprehensive catalogue of his work. He was lucky to have engaged the help of Anita Quilligan Watts, a friend of his and Kathleen's, to assist him with the administrative aspects of his work. Anita was invaluable to him. She helped with the drafting of submissions, with the costing of materials, with site surveys, with drawing up reports, with invoicing and collecting money. She often went with Fred to interview prospective clients, and tempered Fred's sometimes turbulent approach, enough to swing a decision in his favour. And Anita organised his catalogue. I owe her a great debt for her meticulous filing and presentation as I have drawn heavily on her catalogue for the presentation of his work in this chapter.

*Facing page:*
Detail of Draíocht an Ghabha, Tralee, Co Kerry

## Tomás Ághas, *Thomas Ashe*
1967

Fred executed this limestone plaque around the time he finished college. No doubt Domhnall Ó Murchadha was influential in getting him this commission. Located on a pillar at the entrance to GAA Park, Dingle, Co Kerry.

Sos,
*Repose*
1978

Mahogany

101

## Ag Teitheadh, *Flight*
1979

This bronze won awards at both Independent
Artists and Oireachtas exhibitions.

## Ar Dhroim an Domhain,
## *On top of the World*
1981

This piece carved from Kilkenny limestone won an award at the Oireachtas Art Exhibition.

## Norm-Lith
1982

Fred carved this piece from a single block of limestone and envisaged it as a focus for a private garden. The punched surface gives the limestone a more interesting appearance as well as strengthening its tactile qualities.

# Eochal,
## *Metamorphic Bird*
### 1983

Carved from Kilkenny limestone, this was shown at an
exhibition in Marley Park, but
subsequently disappeared and
its whereabouts is still
unknown.

# Casadh Na Gealaí, *The Turning of the Moon*
## 1984

This piece, carved from Dublin granite, was executed in the course of the Sculpture Symposium in Barr na Coille during the summer of 1984. He has commented that the work is based on responses, over time, to the seascapes and landscapes of his native Co. Sligo. It released elements of memory deep in the subconscious. Although abstract, it is founded on that which is familiar. It relates to the soft curved forms of glacial boulders (like the Split Rock in Killeenduff), the horizon separating land from sky and ocean from mountain, the dishing of valleys, the roll and swell of the tide. He wanted the sculpture to become a focus of contemplation, inviting the spectator to travel around it exploring its changing surfaces. He wanted it to possess the elements of continuous change, just like the landscape that inspired it.

## Lawn Crawl
1984

Fred designed this piece specially for the
Outdoor Exhibition of the Independent Artists
held in Marley Park. The material is red deal.

# Sos Sliabh Dá Éan,
## *Tranquillity of Sliabh Dá Éan*
1985

Situated on the shore of Lough Gill the figure of the two birds echoes the outline of the hill on the far side of the lake, Sliabh Daene, the 'mountain of the two birds'. Fred comments on this piece that the suggestion of flight is inherent in the V of the birds' plinth and of the two saddle seats that accompany it; but the atmosphere is of repose, inviting the spectator to sit and contemplate the sculpture, and the mountain of the two birds, and the whole landscape of extraordinary beauty. I don't know if he was conscious that his V is in fact closer to the Tau with all the association of ecstatic worship, Pagan and Christian, implied by that, as I have already outlined. The sculpture was vandalised, but was salvaged by Dr. Siobhán McCormack. The material is Irish oak.

## Samhradh, Samhradh,
*Summer, Summer*
1986

Carved from Sycamore

# Mother and Child

Unfinished. Sculptor's own piece.
Small model in bronze

# Eibhear Alban, *Scottish Granite*
## 1987

This piece was executed at the International Granite Symposium in Kildrummy, Aberdeenshire, Scotland, during the summer of 1987. It was subsequently purchased by Catherine McCann, and brought back to her Shekina Sculpture Garden in Glenmalure, Co. Wicklow. It became a celebrated feature in this garden dedicated to meditation through the contemplation of sculpture.

Fred comments on the creation of this piece:

The materials I use influence my ideas. This granite is millions of years old. It was born in fire, flowed in rivers of liquid lava becoming granite – frozen in time.

I am humbled by this realisation every time I visit a granite quarry – but also excited to see the sun sparkle for the first time on a block freshly released. This is a moment to celebrate in thought and deed. I think of our roots and its association to Scotland. The ancient Celts symbolised life through the Spiral. In this work, I adapt the spiral to granite celebrating continuity, flow, rhythm and unity. It invites you to circle its space to peer into its voids to look over and around it and to touch it.

Catherine McCann comments in her 'Personal view of the Shekina Sculpture Garden':

This is the most dominant sculpture in the collection and this is not by accident. I see it as representing Absolute Mystery – God. Having entered the mystery of oneself, we can then begin to ponder the God question, the origin and ground of all that is. The sculpture, I feel, captures what the artist set out to achieve, namely the notion of immutability and change, a paradox of opposites, very much qualities of a Creator God who is ever the same while remaining full of movement, dynamism, newness, surprise, in the on-going work of creating.

# Fiddler of Dooney
## 1987

Yeats's poem of the same name celebrates the folk character who was reputed to have played his fiddle on the top of Dooney Rock looking out over the beautiful Lough Gill. Comhaltas Ceoltóirí Éireann celebrated Sligo fiddle playing with an award in the name of this folk character and commissioned this bronze as a prize for the winner.

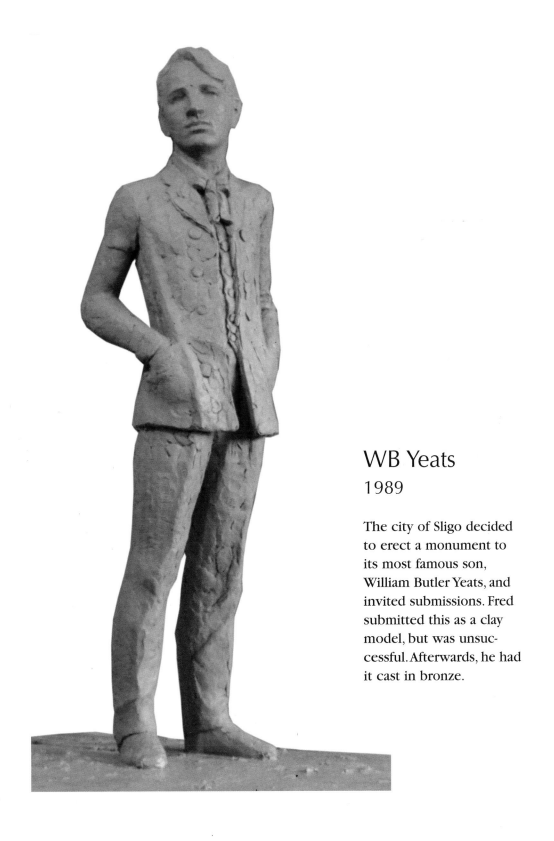

## WB Yeats
### 1989

The city of Sligo decided to erect a monument to its most famous son, William Butler Yeats, and invited submissions. Fred submitted this as a clay model, but was unsuccessful. Afterwards, he had it cast in bronze.

## Tobergeal, *Bright Well*
1989

This is the piece Fred produced for
the Yeat's Workshop, the symposium
to commemorate the fiftieth anniversary of the poet's death

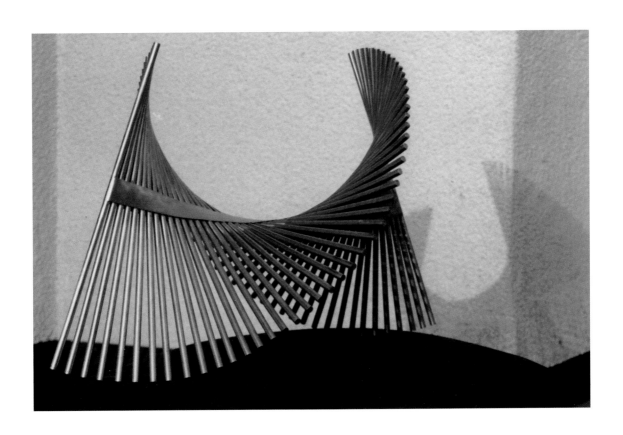

## Spiral
### 1989

This is a model for a large-scale sculpture to be sited on the roundabout at the entrance to Dublin Airport. Aer Rianta invited the submissions and Fred's was on the shortlist. He didn't get the commission, but the short-listed submissions were exhibited in the ILAC Centre. The medium is stainless steel.

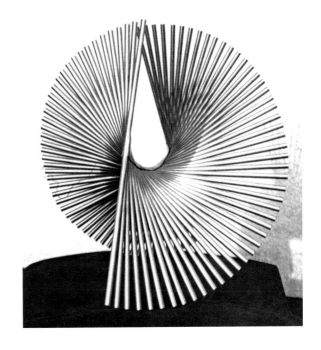

## Turgéis á Bhá, *The Drowning of Turgéis*

This small bronze represents the high king of Ireland, Maelsheachlainn, engaging Turgéis, king of the Norsemen, in single combat. Maelsheachlainn was victorious and is said to have killed his rival by drowning him in Lake Derryvarragh. I am unsure of the date he executed this piece, but he gave it to me as a present around 2000

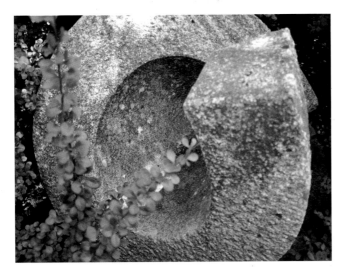

# Roscommon Library
1989

Fred re-visited the spiral motif for this commission. It is sited across the road from the school where I did my Leaving Certificate. And the library was my favourite haunt on Wednesday afternoons when I mitched from sport. The material is granite.

# Armóin,
## *Harmony*
### 1990

In this piece, comissioned by Castlebar Urban Council, Fred had the freedom to create a little landscape including Ice Age boulders. The table and seats with historical motif provide an amenity inviting the observer to come in, sit, use, and become part of the composition. The material is Donegal granite. The location is Thomas Street, Castlebar, Co Mayo.

# Síochháin, *Peace*
## 1991

Fred travelled to India to participate in the International Sculpture Symposium in Cochin in the state of Kerala, South India. Although geographically far-removed from one another, Ireland and India did have strange correspondences that intrigued Fred. Irish, as one of the oldest spoken Indo-European languages was one point of contact. But in Celtic Art there were resonances with Indian Art, for example in the cases of the Castlestrange Stone in Co. Roscommon and the Turoe Stone in Co. Galway. He had also heard of a large dolmen that had existed in Kerala until a hundred years ago when it was unfortunately destroyed. All of this fed into his thought processes as he created this piece out of basalt, shingle, and water. Left is a photo of it being finished, above as it is today, sadly not maintained. The location is Subhash Bose Park in Cochin, Kerala, India.

# Parnell
## 1991

This was Fred's first major commission. To commemorate the centenary of his death, Rathdrum Development Association were opening the Parnell National Park, beside the village, not far from his home in Avondale, and wanted a bronze statue of the statesman as a focus to the park. The figure was to be life-size or greater.

Fred did an enormous amount of research, reading many books to get a sense of his presence, his personality and personal characteristics. In libraries and newspaper offices he studied the photographic records of his appearance, his dress, and the postures he adopted. What he discovered was that Parnell was a very tall man (6ft 3ins) with a striking persona that commanded attention. His presence itself was assertive and commanding, which gained in dignity and force through his low-voiced oratory.

The figure that he created was 8ft 4ins high. It portrayed Parnell as he might have stood amongst his own people in Rathdrum, his arms loosely folded in front, displaying a quiet unease, looking to the right down towards Avondale. Fred saw Parnell as a classic figure and set this pose accordingly.

# Caiseal Óir,
## *Golden Caiseal*
### 1993

This is one of the biggest stone-sculptures in Ireland. When Fred got the commission for a piece of sculpture on the roundabout just beside Bunratty Castle, he certainly had a challenge. It had to be substantial in scale to avoid looking puny in the shadow of the great castle. As always Fred immersed himself in the locality in order to let the concept grow out of the culture and traditions of the area. Here there was a happy coincidence of local stimuli and his personal inclinations. In this corner of Ireland many of the magnificent artefacts of Celtic Art were found – the Ardagh Chalice, the Derrynaflan hoard, but, closer to the site, the great hoard of gold artefacts discovered at Moghane in 1854 during the laying of the West Clare Railway.

Features of the landscape influenced the composition, for example Magh Adhair where the kings of Thomond were crowned. The interior of the sculpture reflected Cahercommaun and became a miniature 'caiseal', or defensive stone fort. But, from the outside, the sculpture takes its shape from the gold gorget or fibula so representative of Celtic Art. The material is limestone and granite.

# Beds
## 1993

Fred was delighted when he got this commission from Dublin Corporation for a piece to enhance a small housing development on Portland Row, a short distance from Seville Place, where he spent many happy years in digs with Mrs McGinn.

He thought that the earthy life of the inner city community was best reflected in the play of the children and the traditional games they acted-out in the streets. He remembered them playing hopscotch and a similar game they called 'beds', where they had to hop and tap an object, usually a shoe-polish tin, with the tip of the toe from one square to the other.

The sculpture is set on the pavement, into which the numbered squares for hopscotch or beds are set. The bronze figures represent two girls chatting while waiting their turn to participate in the game. When he returned after the piece had been sited, Fred was thrilled to find children playing hopscotch on the squares, the two bronze figures among them, as if waiting to join in. When he asked the children what they thought of the two figures, they replied, 'Aw, we love them'. He revealed that he was the sculptor. They mobbed him, 'Aw, Mister, we're always fighting over them. Can you make us another?' It was the kind of critical reaction Fred valued more than any other.

# O'Carolan
## 1994

Turlough O'Carolan, the last of the great traditional harpers of Ireland, was buried in Keadue, on the Roscommon/Leitrim/Sligo border, where his chief patrons the McDermotts were based. Fred modelled the harp on the actual harp of O'Carolan, which was donated to the O'Connors of Ballinagare on his death and is still preserved and displayed in Clonalis House, Castlerea. This commemorative piece was unveiled at the opening of the annual O'Carolan harp festival in 1994 in the village of Keadue. His father, Pat, poses proudly beside Fred.

# Bard of Thomond
## 1994

The late great Jim Kemmy was the one who liaised with Fred on the commission of this commemorative plaque. The simple rectangular slab of limestone with the hand-carved design had to be integrated into the existing head-stone. The decorative motif at the top of the panel represents the Old Thomond Bridge with its 14 arches, so symbolic to the people of Limerick. The location is St Laurence's Cemetery, Limerick.

## Iníon Mhathu, *Mathu's Daughter*
1995

One of the objectives of the Kiltimagh Sculpture Symposium was to create and integrate sculpture in the town parkland settings. Fred's piece
truly achieves this objective by actually incorporating the lawn itself into
his piece. The story of Iníon Mathu, or Mathu's Daughter, dates back to
pre history when the Milesians landed in Éire and drove the Tuatha de
Danann underground. The Milesians inhabited the upper world while
the Tuatha De Danann became the spirit people. They went underground and became the guardians of the fairy forts, raths and liosanna of
Éire. Fred's piece shows Iníon Mathu slowly commencing her descent
into the underworld. The figure is carved from limestone.

# Suigh Liom, *Sit with me*
## 1995

When Fred was commissioned to do a piece for Castlecomer he focused on the coal-mining history of the area. His attention fell on the culm grinders. Local families owned these massive stone wheels that stood up to six feet high. They bought coal cheaply from the local mines, ground them to culm with these wheels, and mixed them with a local yellow clay to make nuggets. These dried 'buns', as they were called locally, burned very effectively.

Fred oriented his sculpture of the culm wheel on the horizontal rather than the vertical to symbolise the decline of the coal industry. The diamond motifs on the side suggest Kilkenny's mineral wealth, the sculpture itself being carved from local limestone.

# Iontas, *Wonder*
## 1989

Fred carved this figure in 1989, immediately after his retirement from teaching. What he was aiming to achieve was a celebration of the mystery of life, the bonding and sense of wonder that exists between mother and child. He was seeking to capture the unspeaking communication that exists between them, that sense of trust, care, and affection. He was aiming for a questioning sense of play, where the joy of the moment is wrapped in hope for the future. Commenting on this piece, he said, 'To appreciate sculpture is to look, to touch, to sense, to learn, and to communicate'. The figure is Donegal granite, the base is Dublin granite. I bought this piece for Lucan Community College in 1995.

## Flute Player

This was a model he submitted for a commission. Fred envisaged a life-size figure on a plinth surrounded by seats that were suggestive of birds alighting. He didn't get the commission and subsequently cast the figure of the girl in bronze.

# In Ómós Don Ind, *Homage to India*
## 1996/7

Fred made two visits to India to participate in Sculpture Symposia. He was greatly taken with Indian culture, rooted in age-old tradition, rich in the symbolic interpretation and explanation of life. This piece is a tribute to India and to the inspiration it provided him. The material is limestone.

## Ní Mar a Shíltear Bítear, *Things are not as they seem*
1996

This piece is ideally located in the Shekina Sculpture Garden, a small park created by Catherine McCann in Glenmalure, Co Wicklow, to stimulate peaceful meditation by contemplating the different pieces of sculpture on display. Fred explains his use of the Irish 'sean fhocal' as a title in that he is seeking to create harmony out of opposites and contradictions.

Catherine McCann comments in her 'Personal View of the Shekina Sculpture Garden':

– The first sculpture in this story is oneself – the human person. We must begin with our own experience, and the fundamental human experience is that we question, and even question our own questioning. 'Things are not what they seem', the artist says, and our personal challenge in coming to an understanding of reality is to query, 'is it so?' This piece is the opener, it invites you to ponder your own questioning as you look and reflect –.

# Ladder and Hose
## 1996

When Fred got the commission to provide a piece of sculpture for the new Fire Station in Strokestown, Co Roscommon, he fixed on the fireman's ladder and hose as representative images. The material is limestone.

## Draíocht na Spéire,
### *The Magic of the Sky*
1996

This piece won the prestigious Waterford Crystal Award
when it was shown in the Oireachtas Art Exhibition in
1996. He was using the conflicting mathematical forms,
circles, squares, triangles, to create directional interplay
and movement suggestive of celestial rotation. The
material is limestone and basalt.

# Gulbarga
1996

This piece was made as part of a sculpture symposium held in Gulbarga city in Karmataka in India. The material is basalt.

## Solas Iontach, *Light Wonder*
1996

Fred produced this at the Sculpture Symposium in Nanao City, Japan. The brief was to create sculpture with light as an integral part of the design. This triggered thoughts of Newgrange for Fred, with the sun entering the subterranean chamber for a brief period at the Winter Solstice. Traditional western sculpture presumes light coming from an external source, normally the sun, to light up the external surfaces of the piece. But the Japanese were using light as a factor in the work itself, for example illuminating the piece from within. Fred's design combined both: his piece had all the appearance of a traditional stone sculpture in daylight, but in darkness was illuminated from below to manifest other aspects and create a totally different impact on the eye.

Fred's comment on the Symposium:

I was invited by the Mayor of Nanao City, Japan, to participate in the 1997 stone sculpture symposium which was held at Komaruyama Park, 16th July – 16th August 1997. I was one of two international artists invited to participate, representing Ireland, with Mary Bourne representing Scotland. This Symposium was the third to have taken place in Nanao. It was part of a long-term project to create public sculpture for an urban environment in conjunction with city planning. In this regard it was unique to Japan and was being conducted as a pilot project by the City of Nanao. The material is grey granite.

# The Parthalonians
## 1997

When commissioned to do a sculpture for Ballyshannon, Co Donegal, Fred drew his concept from the tradition that the Parthalonians were the first people to reach Ireland and settled in the Erne valley. So the two figures are the leader Parthalon and his wife Parthalonia. They stand like two megaliths but with a hint of their Mediterranean origins in the features. There is a narrative contained in the dynamic between the two figures and the sleeping dog at their feet. Parthalon went hunting one morning, promising to be back before dark, and leaving Parthalonia with her pet dog Saimer. The hunting was good and Parthalon did not return for four days. He was greeted by a furious and jealous wife who accused him of being with another woman. The row intensified until Parthalon lost his self-control and, seeing her pet dog curled at her feet, lashed out and killed the poor animal. The material is limestone.

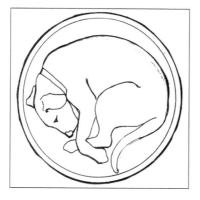

# Faoin Sceach, *Under the Hawthorn*
## 1997

Fred was commissioned to do this bronze sculpture to commemorate
the Great Famine of 150 years earlier. He chose the image of the 'sceach'
or lone thorn bush, familiar but haunting, to signify the awful fate of the
nameless dead buried in this graveyard adjacent to the old Workhouse
on the outskirts of Sligo town. The 'sceach' was sacred to the people of
the underworld, the dead, and the sidhe, in Irish folklore and could not
be disturbed despite any inconvenience its location might cause. Fred
envisaged his bronze tree as a marker and suitable memorial to the
unfortunate people buried underneath.

# Altar and Font
## 1997

When he got this commission, for the Catholic Church in Carnlough, Co Antrim, Fred thought long and hard on how it should be executed. His conclusion was that they should not be ornamented in any way that would distract from the ritual for which they were intended. He created simple forms that would attract the eye and focus it on the location where the important events would take place. The material is granite.

# 1798 Memorial
## 1998

Such was the success of the Parnell statue that the people of Rathdrum, Co Wicklow, invited Fred back to do a second memorial in the town, a memorial to the 1798 Rebellion. He had returned from Japan full of enthusiasm for internal lighting. The location was on a height, so he started with the concept of the fire-beacon used by the rebels. The voids in the four granite slabs are shaped into flames symbolising passionate rebellion, on two sides; on the other two sides they are shaped into pikes, the weapons associated with the Rebellion.

## Draíocht an Ghabha,
### *The Magic of the Blacksmith*
1998

When he was commissioned to provide a sculpture for the park in Tralee adjacent to the Siamsa Tire Theatre, Fred explains why he chose the Blacksmith: I chose the Blacksmith as a symbol of the people of North Kerry. The Smith was grounded through his tenacity and wisdom with his community. Like the Alchemist he practised a semi-magical craft. Using the earth symbols of Air, Fire and Water he provided an industry which served the Community. His knowledge, learning and medicine he shared with the people whom he served. As distributor of local folklore, of storytelling, song and 'craic' he fulfilled a need to those who gathered round the glow of the furnace similar to the television or the media of today. The beat or rhythm of his hammer on anvil has been an inspiration for poets and musicians. The people of Tralee have adapted the unique forging tap of the blacksmith and have immortalised the spirit of his rhythm in dance. The material is limestone.

# Bull, Bear, Stag
## 1998

Fred was invited by the financier, Dermot Desmond, to submit a proposal for a major piece of sculpture to be placed outside the International Financial Services Centre in Dublin. Fred suggested forms of the bull, bear, and stag, terms used to describe different phases of the market in the Stock Exchange. This was agreed and he proceeded to develop the concept to the wax model stage. Again there was general acclaim and great enthusiasm for the proposal. Unfortunately that was as far as it went and the figures were never realised in full scale.

# Boffin Street
## 1999

The quayside location of this commission suggested the concept of bollards. Boffin Street in Westport was associated with the people sailing to and from Inishboffin. The quays were also a centre of commerce and milling. So Fred created three bollards carved with relief panels, a map of Inishboffin, quayside Mills, and a sailing boat. Water motifs abound, and the band of hearts represent, would you believe, a local soccer team called Quay Hearts. The material is limestone.

# 1916-1923 Memorial
## 2000

This monument, located in Kennedy Parade, Sligo, commemorating the people who died during that troubled period of our history from 1916 to 1923 is laden with symbolic narrative. The table-top represents Ireland divided by the inlaid sword, but united by the handshake of reconciliation. The four supporting columns are the four provinces, while the six seats represent the six baronies of County Sligo. The material is granite. Fred envisaged the trees planted to the rear of the site as an integral part of the design, symbolising the growth of the new nation.

# Cois Cuan, *By the Harbour*
## 1999

This sculpture celebrates the opening of the new Boyle Harbour and
Canal in Co Roscommon. The elements of the Sculpture are assembled as
if they were relics of a bygone age, images redolent of the old inland
waterways. They appear tilting, as if subsiding into the earth, their studied casualness inviting people to gather and banter. The material is
Kilkenny limestone.

# Millennium Sculpture
## 2000

The brief for this sculpture, which I commissioned for Lucan
Community College, was to produce a piece for an internal school courtyard which would celebrate the advent of the new Millennium. Fred was
still excited by his Japan experience and keen to experiment with internal lighting. The two upright columns and the three horizontal bowls or
fonts symbolise the two millennia becoming three. The embedded light
under the sculpture represents Christianity shining up through voids in
the first two horizontals touching the base of the third. The material is
limestone

# Foinse Gheal,
## *Light Fountain*
2001

Fred has left a detailed account of the thinking that went into this piece which was commissioned by Comhar Linn, the INTO Credit Union, for the garden of their premises at 33 Parnell Square, Dublin:

The mathematics behind this sculpture is based on one of the most influential architects of the 20th century. He devised a system of scaling based on the measure of man. In devising this modular system he changed in many respects spatial relationships. I admire and acknowledge the theories of Le Corbusier.

These were the thoughts which formulated my concept for the sculpture Foinse Gheal. Like Le Corbusier, I wish to acknowledge the skill of man and humanity as the springboard for the future, and comparable symbols with INTO came to mind.

When I think of education, I think of fonts of knowledge. These fonts are the dishes from which the spirit and mind of man are illuminated and which permeate in all directions. They guide us, show us the way, give us strength of character.

This sculpture has the fonts of knowledge as its foundation. The granite column is a classical form. It symbolises civilisation and stability.

This column is a symbol of the organisation of INTO. Nothing can be more earthly than granite, particularly our own granite. The granite column symbolises the spine, the backbone of our beginning. This symbol can be viewed in its many diverse connotations. It can be seen as being the spine on which primary education hinges.

Illumination is a primary element within this sculpture. It represents the flow of knowledge between each font. The granite column is segmented yet joined together. Though separate in its many elements the light shines its remembrance of the many individuals who have participated in the INTO organisation and also illuminates the way forward for ongoing continuity. It symbolises the stem on which all growth is based.

This sculpture is celebratory in the sense that it acknowledges our realisation of time and our place in time. This sculpture celebrates the beginning of our entry into the 3rd millennium. Light has easily passed through the last two, the light is only beginning to break to the third. Perhaps in a thousand years, the cap from this sculpture can be removed and a further font can be placed in accordance with its sense of nearness to this the beginning of the third millennium.

## Margaret of New Orleans
2002

This plaque was commissioned for the Health Centre in Carrigallen to celebrate a local woman who emigrated to New Orleans and became a legend in that city for her good work, particularly looking after orphans. This is the clay model, but it was cast in bronze.

# Clonard Road
2003/4

These four bronze wall reliefs were commissioned by Dublin City
Council for a housing project in Poddle Close, off Clonard Road in the
South-Dublin suburb of Kimmage, Dublin.

# Hop Skip and Jump
## 2003

When Fred received this commission for a park in Clash, Abbeyfeale, Co Limerick, he was again preoccupied with creating sculpture with which the viewers can interact, in which they can be active. He explains his concept for this piece:

Consideration of the needs of the whole community - adults, children and apartment tenants is a key element within this design concept.

On one level the design is child oriented relating back to street games of hopscotch, skipping ropes and jumping games. The fundamental shapes of a square, triangle and circle have also been encompassed into the design. My

concern with designing a feature that allows for creative interaction with children has also focused on minimising hazards. The elements that appear as children's seats are designed to create the minimum vertical focus.

The design beckons you to walk into its space, to travel its surface and edge, to play, to sense, to touch to peer into and ponder. For a child it should be a place of wonder, imagination and play. For an adult, it should be a place of remembrance and reflection. As you leave, it should invite you to return another time so that it can communicate further. The material is limestone.

# Ré na Mara,
## *Moon of the Sea*
### 2004/5

This was Fred's last sculpture. Commissioned for a private garden in Rosses Point, it is oriented to focus on Queen Maeve's cairn on top of Knocknarea across Sligo Bay. This significant alignment is in keeping with the Neolithic monuments of the Sligo landscape, many of which are aligned to the heavenly bodies at specific and significant moments. Knocknarea itself, 'the mountain of the moon', was Sligo's holiest mountain in the pre-Christian era. By strange and happy coincidence Fred's own home and studio in Strandhill are within the same alignment. The material is Kilkenny limestone.

# Chapter 7

# Illness and Death

On 18th May, 2004, I was giving a reading in the village of Easkey. I had arranged with Fred that we would meet afterwards for a drink and a chat. I was looking forward to that. It was my first time to do a reading in Easkey, and it was linked to a commission I had received to write a novel based on my childhood experiences. This time it was I had the commission and he was enthusiastically helping me to reconnect with our shared history. But in the middle of the reading my mobile phone rang. Apologising sheepishly to my audience, I took the phone out to knock it off. But when I saw it was Fred, I supposed that he just wanted to arrange when and where we would meet. So with the amused agreement of the audience, I took the call. But it wasn't Fred on the line, it was Kathleen, to say Fred couldn't meet me, that he was in the hospital in Sligo. She sounded upset, and I couldn't talk in front of my audience, so I said I would call on him the next morning.

Around 11.00 the next day I approached the main door of the hospital and saw Fred loitering outside puffing away at a cigarette. I was relieved.

"What's the matter?" I asked.

"I was a bit dizzy, so I have to get tests. Inflamation of the brain or something like that."

I shivered, but tried to appear casual. "When are the tests?"

"Whenever they have a bed for me in Beaumont. I don't want to be hanging around here in the mean time, so I'm trying to get home. Come on, we'll see if I can get discharged, and you can drive me back to Strandhill."

I drove him home, and when I saw that his family was gathering, I suspected the news was worse than Fred realised. I was right. When I had a

*Facing page:*
Detail of Cois Cuan, Boyle, Co Roscommon

private word with Kathleen she told me it was a tumour.

A few days later I was back in Dublin when Kathleen phoned to say Fred was in Beaumont and was in a very bad condition. I hurried across. I could scarcely believe what I saw. Fred was almost in a coma and appeared physically helpless. And he seemed to be fading fast. It was one of the most frightening experiences of my life. However, the doctors were re-assuring us that he was in no immediate danger. He looked in immediate danger to me. But the doctors were right. The paralysis was caused by a swelling of the tumour, and they were able to stabilise this with steroids. However, Fred was never to be his old self again. They operated and removed as much of the tumour as they could, but gave him nine months to live.

Two years earlier at the funeral of one of his elder sisters, Fred had said to me, "I'm next".

"What do you mean?"

"I'm next. I'm the oldest now."

It was something I hadn't reflected on, even though it was such a stark fact. He was the eighth in a family of ten and all his older siblings were now gone. Many had died very young, and many of cancer. He looked as if he was seriously considering his position as next in line.

"Fred, you will live to be a hundred. There is a law of averages, and if the rest of them died young, the three of you that are left will live long and live healthy. Look at my father's family."

It was true. My father was one of nine, and six of his siblings died young, mostly in their thirties. But the three that were left lived into old age.

"Maybe. We'll see."

But Fred was to be proved right. He was next in line and fate was not to relent.

We all wonder how we would cope if handed such a sentence. And if I had been asked how Fred would cope, my prediction would have been totally askew. He accepted the sentence with dignity, even with serenity, but with a fierce determination to defy fate, to beat the disease. And he was totally optimistic that he could and would do so.

His operation gave him some ease, but very little mobility back. He was confined to the wheelchair and had no power in his left hand or arm. He struggled for control over his right hand, but insisted on lighting his cigarette unaided. Smoking was a pleasure he clung to right to the end. When they did a CAT scan and told him his lungs were completely free of cancer he felt vindicated in his indulgence.

Yes, he accepted his cross with uncharacteristic serenity. There was no venting of frustration, no cursing his luck. He was deeply affected by the love and care he got from everybody, from his family and friends, from the caring personnel, from total strangers.

Fate was cruel. There were so many factors in his life that were merging into what should have been a happily productive period for Fred. His family was just about reared. He was converting the stables his father had built at the cottage in Killeenduff into a comfortable well-equipped studio where he could work at ease whenever he wanted. Within the arts community in the North West he was deeply admired and respected as an artist and as a man.

But the most significant factor contributing to this sense of equilibrium in his life was his involvement in the Sculpture Centre in Manorhamilton. For many years he had been executing his large stone sculptures in the Feelystone workshops in Boyle, where they provided him with the stone, the space, and the equipment. He enjoyed a warm sympathetic relationship with Barry Feely, the owner and director of the company. I had visited him several times there, especially when he was working on the Millennium Sculpture for Lucan.

But when the Sculpture Centre in Manorhamilton came into being, powered by Fred's former student and now close friend, Jackie McKenna, he was offered the use of space and equipment for his work. He accepted. They had casting facilities, so he was able to do bronze reliefs, Margaret of New Orleans and the four plaques for Clonard Road. He also executed there the abstract stone sculpture, Ré na Mara.

It was different to Feelystone, where he worked alone or with occasional assistance. In Manorhamilton there was a community of artists working in a wide range of media. Within this community there were trainees, learning the various arts and crafts. So when Fred was working on something he had assistants who were there to help but also to learn. Fred was delighted to be imparting his knowledge to these acolytes, and settled into the role of the master with his apprentices around him. It struck me that the wheel had come full circle, and here was he, in the exact role Murphy had played in his life so long before, master, revered figure, storyteller, inspiring his young disciples with a love and a passion for art, while at the same time entertaining them with yarns and anecdotes.

Fred was still at the peak of his artistic powers despite no longer being able for the arduous hand-carving of stone. And it seemed that he would settle into a mellow, peaceful, but productive era, as a master in the style of his revered Renaissance artists.

Back in Killeenduff I had bought the cottage that I had been born in and that had been out of family hands for forty years. We were anticipating being next-door neighbours once more, both drawing inspiration from the landscape and the community in which we had grown up, enjoying each other's company into old age.

But we were never once to meet in Killeenduff again as next-door neighbours. When he was in St Luke's in Dublin getting his radium treatment, I generally went in at lunch time to see him and to take him out for his smoke. The wonderful and devoted Orla and Elaine had reorganised their working days, so that one of them came in early in the morning to help him with his breakfast, the other in the evening to look after him for his dinner. Wheeling him around the grounds, we indulged in nostalgia, recalling incidents from our childhood, the newly baked buns we stole off windows where they had been left to cool, the tricks we played on our neighbours at Hallowe'en. And then Fred would suddenly stare at a corner of the grounds and outline rapidly a plan for turning it into a sculpture garden.

In Manorhamilton, Fred's most remarkable apprentice was Sam McGee. He mentioned him to me on many occasions as a young man who had a definite talent for sculpture and was coming to it late but coming with great enthusiasm and dedication. He mentioned him, and regularly updated me on his progress, because Sam's father was from our own locality, outside the village of Dromore West, and I knew the family very well. Sam's father, Stuart, was a Minister in the Church of Ireland and had lived away from Co. Sligo much of his working life, but was now back in Strandhill about half a mile from Fred's house. Sam had settled in England after college, had married, and had two children. However, his marriage broke up and, deeply distraught, he returned to Ireland and was living with Stuart and his mother, Eunice. This was when he decided to explore his life-long ambition and try his hand at art. He heard of Manorhamilton and enrolled as a trainee under their FAS programme. He was in his late thirties by then. And he was assigned to Fred.

Fred was enthusiastic about Sam's talent and impressed by his dedication. On top of that Sam had a wonderful, bright, cheerful personality, radiating warmth and good will. Fred was delighted to be coaching him and Sam was obviously very happy to have such a mentor.

When Fred returned to Strandhill after his treatment, Sam was a daily

visitor, checking if there was anything needed, anything he could do. Eventually there was a formal arrangement that Sam came early every morning and looked after Fred until lunchtime, when a nurse, Mitzie, took over in the afternoon for a few hours until Kathleen came home from work. Both Sam and Mitzie, who was a poet, were wonderful presences in Fred's life during his illness, contributing to his emotional equilibrium, coaxing him into good humour, even on the darkest days. They, along with the quiet supportive presence of Pauric who had re-organised his life to spend time at his father's side, gave the home a sense of calm amid the constant flow of visitors.

From the beginning of his illness, Fred came to terms with the dissolution of his physical powers in a remarkably philosophical way. He estimated that the new limitations would allow him at best to draw and paint. He enlisted the help of Sam and of his youngest son, Finn, who was now an art student himself, studying design in college. They helped to set him up with all the materials he needed and every day organised him in front of his easel. With slow and patient strokes, Fred began to paint.

Even though his physical powers were limited to an excruciating degree,

Sam, Fred and Mitzie photographed on the day 'Ré na Mara' was sited in Rosses Point

173

Fred's mind was as expansive and ambitious as ever. He began to think in terms of orchestrating a major installation to represent what had happened to him, a multi-media work centred on the painting he was working on. He wanted to include a video of an operation to remove a brain tumour and another video that RTE had made showing him working on his last stone sculpture, Ré na Mara, in the Manorhamilton Sculpture Centre. On another screen he visualised a sequence of still photographs of his sculpture from around the country. He intended another sequence of still photographs of the carers who surrounded him. He asked me if I would write a poem or a song to be included. Central to all of this was the painting he was working on and its symbolism.

The painting was of the slaying of Balor, a major figure in Irish mythology. Balor was the great warrior of the Fomorians, portrayed as a pirate people inhabiting the North West of Ireland, but mainly Donegal and Tory Island. Balor had some awesome weapons in his armoury, chief among them an eye in the centre of his forehead, which, when opened, could kill everyone it looked upon. He was also endowed with invincibility in so far as he could be killed only by one of his own progeny. He was a formidable asset to the Fomorians who were under threat from the newly arrived people, the Tuatha De Dannan. The new arrivals had already subjugated the Fir Bolg who had previously controlled the rest of the country, and moved north west to engage the Fomorians in the epic battle of Moytura on the slopes of the Bricklieve Mountain in Co. Sligo.

Balor had tried to ensure his invincibility in the wake of the prophecy by locking up his only daughter in a tower so that he would never have progeny to slay him. But, as happens in such stories, a chap came by, fell for the daughter, managed to gain access, and when the resultant child was born they smuggled him out of the tower. Later, the army of the Tuatha De Dannan, advancing against the Fomorians at Moytura, was led by a young warrior-hero, Lugh. He was none other than this baby grown to manhood, and he slew his grandfather by piercing the evil eye with his spear.

Fred drew the analogy between Balor being slain by his progeny and his own body being attacked by its cells. The graphic expressionistic painting that emerged was fraught with the grotesque horror of it all. Yet I could see little other than that in the analogy. Balor was the archetypal destroyer, Lugh the archetypal creator, and so I pitched my poem at a rejection of Fred's analogy.

# Not Balor, Lugh

*for Fred Conlon, Sculptor*

No Balor you
although by name a dark Fomorian
struck struck struck down
by that shaft
that cruel cunning shaft
launched
not by some fortuitous bowman on the hill
but by the flesh of your own flesh
the treacherous patricidal shaft
of your own substance.

The Slaying of
Balor

And yet
you are not Balor
you are not of the withering north.
Balor's fearsome eye
the one set in the centre of his skull
spread winter death and desolation.
No
your mind's eye
benign
like an internal sun
shed naught
but light and life and generosity.

Yes
more Lugh
the multi-skilled
whose powers were honed
in communion with the sea
wielder of the long rays
slayer of winter
upon the epic fields
where you
drew inspiration
from a cleft boulder
the cast-aside token
of the anger of a demi-god.

Like Lugh
you mastered
arts and crafts
began by righting
the defects
of a bauble in a shop window
and proceeded
to release the beauty
the Creator had immured
in blocks of ancient stone.

When I emailed the poem to him, I got the following reply from Fred, through Kathleen.

30 January, 2005

*Jack's poem arrives at 7pm by email.*

*I want you to read this for the film next time that there is a voice recording… (Tear filled eyes as Kathleen reads it to Fred x 3)*

*I think that it is poetic.*

*It fits in with what is being done – it expresses the attack within my own system. It is poetic and expressive of where I am at.*

*It shows that it is written by someone who knows me very well.*

*Ar scáth a chéile a mhairimid.*

*We were all dependent on each other when we were in Killeenduff. No scone was safe on any windowsill when we grew up. It took the village to raise the child.*

*The poem needs to be spoken.*

*I want to smile, but I can't. I cry instead.*

*Does there have to be some explanation of the Split Rock Stone? Nobody else but you Jack could read it.*

*I would like to say I am flattered by it. I would like Lolly to write the story about the Split Rock.*

*Míle Buíochas*

*Fred*

Frank Conway, a long-time friend of Fred's, agreed to help him with the video aspect of the installation, and spent some time filming Fred as he modelled a head in clay. Finn and Sam put enormous effort into organising other aspects of the installation. But as the weeks passed and Fred's condition deteriorated it became obvious that he would not manage to complete it. Then he became fretful that he would be letting down all the people who had been helping if he were to fail in bringing it to completion.

But after Fred's death, Frank Conway did salvage an element of the project. He simplified Fred's concept into a very powerful video-based installation entitled 'Become', an extremely moving exploration of the experience of illness and its effect on the mind, body, and perception of an artist, a fitting salute to Fred's indomitable creativity.

During his illness, Fred continued to keep his engagements and oversaw the siting of 'Ré na Mara' in Rosses Point. He attended the unveiling of the plaques in Clonard Road. And one night when I was giving a reading in the Colemen Centre in Gorteen, who came through the door in his wheelchair but Fred! His love of life, love of people, love of art in all its forms was passionate to the end.

My last goodbye to Fred before he slipped into coma took place in his sitting room where he was propped in front of the easel, his brush in his right hand. He had managed to get a touch of paint onto the tip of the brush and with enormous effort he applied it to the picture in front of him.

A few days later Kathleen called to say he was sinking rapidly. I said I would go down the following morning. But later that evening Orla rang to say that Vonnie, the much-loved and much-loving G.P. who looked after Fred throughout his illness, was of the opinion that Fred wouldn't make it through the night. I got into the car, and was in Strandhill three hours later.

Fred's breathing was coming in gasps. He had developed pneumonia and his lungs were slowly filling up. In the early hours of the morning, Fred passed away, surrounded by his family and close friends. Niall had arrived from London and played the musical piece 'Lifetime', he had composed for Fred.

It was the 24th of February. In his last weeks he had asked the date as soon as he woke up every morning. And when he heard it wasn't the 24th he was relieved. He was obsessed by the 24th, as many of his family had died on that exact day of different months, and he had an intuition that he would too.

There were many forebodings, but only recognised in retrospect, of course. In 2001 I had been organising an arts programme for Airfield House in Dundrum, Dublin. It occurred to me that it would be fascinating to bring Fred and his circle of friends from his College of Art days together for an exhibition. They had exhibited together in group shows up to the late sixties, but afterwards they went their separate ways, their paths had not crossed again. I was the only one who maintained contact with all of them.

So I brought them together to discuss mounting a group exhibition. The 'meeting' took place in a pub where a few pints stripped away the layers of experience that thirty years of life had applied, and we were back reminiscing about college days and the sixties, and interjecting quick briefings on what had happened in our lives since then.

Henry Sharpe had continued his steadfast commitment to painting, working part-time as a lecturer of drawing in the National College of Art and Design, as it was now called. He was producing a constant stream of work and had no problem committing himself to this exhibition. Neither had John Walsh, who had moved back to Tipperary when he finished in college and had been teaching there down through the years. Aidan Hickey, on the other hand, did have a problem. He had gone to Hornsey College of Art in London in the early seventies to study film animation and had specialised in animation ever since, so he hadn't stood in front of an easel for thirty years. However, he promised he would go to Kennedys in Harcourt Street without delay, purchase his supplies, and have two paintings ready for the exhibition. Denis Bannister had opted for architecture as a profession, and had spent the years lecturing in that subject in the Dublin Institute of Technology. He had continued painting, mostly in watercolour, but his output was numerically limited. However he committed himself to having at least two drawings ready for the exhibition. Fred, I knew, had a number of small bronzes ready for show. So, with everyone committed and a date settled, the exhibition moved from proposal to fixture, and Henry came up with the name, Quinque, 'five'.

But of course there was an empty chair at the table. Donal Byrne had abandoned his studies at the College of Art and, having taken the old Matriculation examination, he enrolled in University College Dublin to study History of Art. He had a distinguished career in that field, specialising in medieval illuminated manuscripts, and spent many years lecturing in Aberdeen University. He had lost touch with all of us, so it was a shock when the first report we heard was of his suicide.

The Quinque exhibition was a success, but the pub-meetings before and after provided the most pleasure. At the final get-together there was a sense of people once again going off to follow their own trajectories. Fred took two things out of his bag. One was a book, and he handed it to Aidan. "I borrowed that from you a while ago," he said with a laugh. Aidan looked at it. Whitman's 'Leaves of Grass'. He laughed. "Yes, about forty years ago, and would you believe I do remember that book". The other was a small black folder, and he handed it to me. "You gave me that to read one time and I never gave it back". I opened it to find that it was a copy of all the poems that I had written in my teenage years. I certainly didn't remember giving it to him but I was pleased to have it back, because I had no copy of the juvenilia other than the ones that had been published. I remember being struck by this squaring of accounts, as if Fred was anticipating we might not all be together again.

Another mysterious coincidence was the fate of the beloved Sam McGee, who had nursed Fred as a mother or brother would have done. Sam became ill a few months after Fred died. He was diagnosed as having the exact same tumour as Fred. But when he was offered the same course of treatment as Fred, he declined. No operation, no treatment. Sam saw the sustained agony of Fred and his family, and opted for a quick exit instead. Sam died just months after Fred and we laid him to rest in the little Church of Ireland cemetery attached to his father's church in Strandhill.

Fred was buried in the cemetery in Easkey among his family and relatives, among all the characters we listened to with awe when we were children. I think of them as twilight gathers huddling in the darkness to light their cigarettes and settle in to a night of storytelling, of exchanging jokes, of comparing achievements on the bog or in the hayfield, or at pulling the black wrack from the tide in the depth of winter.

Over Fred's grave is a very beautiful sculpture by his former student, close friend, fellow sculptor, Eileen McDonagh.

Fred's grave in Roslea Cemetery near Easkey. The sculpture is by Eileen McDonagh

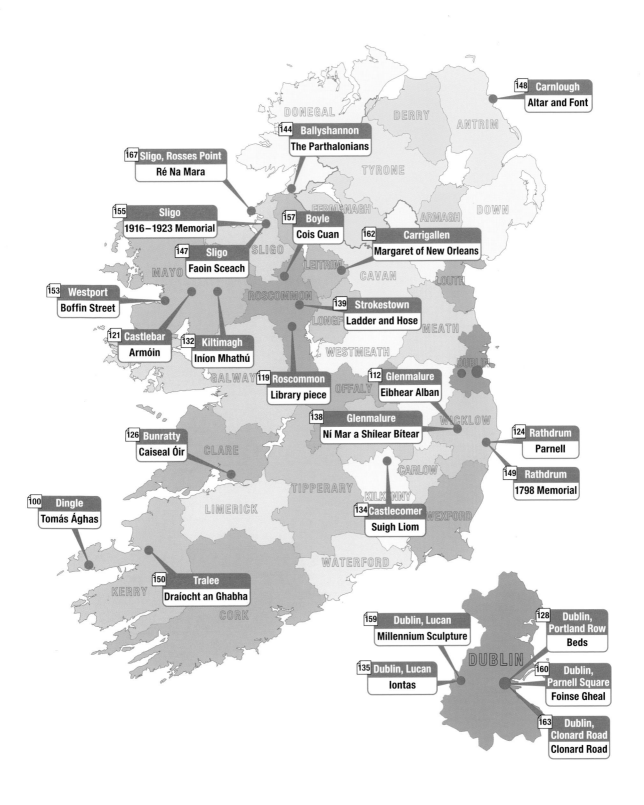

148 Carnlough
Altar and Font

144 Ballyshannon
The Parthalonians

167 Sligo, Rosses Point
Ré Na Mara

155 Sligo
1916–1923 Memorial

157 Boyle
Cois Cuan

162 Carrigallen
Margaret of New Orleans

147 Sligo
Faoin Sceach

153 Westport
Boffin Street

139 Strokestown
Ladder and Hose

121 Castlebar
Armóin

132 Kiltimagh
Iníon Mhathú

119 Roscommon
Library piece

112 Glenmalure
Eibhear Alban

138 Glenmalure
Ní Mar a Shílear Bítear

124 Rathdrum
Parnell

126 Bunratty
Caiseal Óir

149 Rathdrum
1798 Memorial

100 Dingle
Tomás Ághas

134 Castlecomer
Suigh Liom

150 Tralee
Draíocht an Ghabha

159 Dublin, Lucan
Millennium Sculpture

128 Dublin, Portland Row
Beds

135 Dublin, Lucan
Iontas

160 Dublin, Parnell Square
Foinse Gheal

163 Dublin, Clonard Road
Clonard Road